# Will You Murder Your African American Children?

## A Challenge to Parental Caregivers

by William R. Manson

DORRANCE PUBLISHING CO., INC.
PITTSBURGH, PENNSYLVANIA 15222

*All Rights Reserved*
Copyright © 1994 by William R. Manson
No part of this book may be reproduced or transmitted in any form or by any means, electronic or mechanical, including photocopying, recording, or by any information storage and retrieval system without permission in writing from the publisher.

ISBN # 0-8059-3560-6
Printed in the United States of America

*First Printing*

For information or to order additional books, please write:
Dorrance Publishing Co., Inc.
643 Smithfield Street
Pittsburgh, Pennsylvania 15222
U.S.A.

Dedicated to

*Baba Jundae Vaughn*

Baba wisely convinced me to deliver my message to a specific audience and not to attempt to impress critics and other writers.

# Table of Contents

Introduction ........................................................................... vii

Section 1: *Decisions* ............................................................. 1
    A. Attention
    B. Listening
Section 2: *Hugs and Kisses* .................................................. 3
    A. Say, I Love You
    B. Honesty
Section 3: *Self-Presentation* ................................................. 7
    A. Health
    B. Profanity
    C. Firmness
    D. Convictions
    E. Bad Habits
Section 4: *Discipline* ............................................................ 9
    A. Religion
    B. Failures
    C. Teachers
    D. Negative Behavior
    E. Positive Reinforcement
Section 5: *Sports* ................................................................ 15
Section 6: *Nutrition* ............................................................ 17
Section 7: *Fighting* ............................................................. 29
    A. Schematic Design
    B. Research
Section 8: *African American Male Sexuality* ...................... 47

Glossary ............................................................................... 61

# Introduction

Parents and guardians want their children to grow up in a safe, secure, and educated environment. When their children leave their homes, for any reason, parents want to be comfortable in the thought that they will be safe. They want their children to be well-educated—engineers, lawyers, doctors, teachers. In short, they want the best of everything for their children.

Well, parents, welcome to the real world. In order for you to secure for your children all of the things you want for them, you have to work. You have to work harder than ever before. And they must come first in everything, absolutely everything.

Most of the reasons for parents failing their children will be discussed in later chapters, but before we begin I think we should discuss the three reasons close to this author (they will be discussed later in detail).

Number one is the lack of parenting skills. Quite a few African Americans don't know how to be parents. And they are too proud or just too dumb to seek help. They oftentimes feel that they should raise their children just as they were raised. That is not always true. This is a skill that is learned through many avenues: books, school, trial and error, church, parenting organizations, and of course, home. The methods can change from generation to generation, from year to year, from month to month, from week to week, from day to day, from hour to hour, and from minute to minute. The many types of individuals create the need for many changes in styles of lessons and modes of teaching. Children are people, and their attitudes, behaviors, and temperaments vary. The lessons learned could be good or bad and something should be gained from both. The good things should be taken in and improved on, and the bad things should serve as warnings and be eliminated.

Number two, I think the greatest harm done to African American children was integration. Some African American parents thought that integration was going to be the cure-all for their children. They seemed to think that when their children went to school with white children, they would learn more and they would be absolved of all educational responsibilities for their children. They soon learned that white children also had educational problems and they needed help as much as the African American children. As this integration process continued, there was a total destruction of some great African American schools.

Some scholars argue that the difference in the rate of success of whites in all-white schools compared to the rate of success of African Americans in African American schools were the supplies, facilities, and qualified teachers. I beg to differ on that point. If a child goes to school to learn and nothing else, he or she can learn in an outhouse.

African Americans have to take care of their own children. They cannot continue to follow the white population from school setting to school setting. For example the African American parents sent their children to Catholic schools to be with white children to obtain a better education. For the most part, the white parents took their children out of Catholic schools and put them in private schools. The African American parents followed by placing their children in private schools. Once again the white parents took their children out of private schools and formed academies. And the educational chase continues.

I really don't think chasing white people from educational facility to educational facility will improve African American education. Parents should notice that nothing has changed for the betterment of African American education. Despite so-called integration, African American education is at an all-time low. Parents should build their own schools and communities and not depend on others to do it for them.

Number three, education in human sexuality is an almost forgotten art (discussed in a later chapter). African American children are thrown out into society without the most rudimentary knowledge about what sex is really all about. Oftentimes they perform (without true knowledge) the intercourse part, but they know nothing about developing a long-lasting, meaningful relationship with one partner. Their knowledge of love, sharing, and caring is occasionally misguided.

There are times when this lack of sexual knowledge can cause anxiety, frustration, anger, and oftentimes violence.

Caregivers, read this book and glean whatever you can from it.

# Section 1
*Decisions*

A. Attention
B. Listening

Decisions are customarily made according to the outcomes that you desire. Outcomes are frequently successful according to the intensity in which you pursue a desired goal.

There is very little difference when you are raising children. It goes back to the old adage, "Pay me now or pay me later." This means that if you do not do the right things concerning the nurturing of your children in their formative years, your payment may be excessive visits to schools for disciplinary reasons, unwanted visits to the courts and jails, undesirable visits to maternity wards, unwanted attempts at physical confrontations, and perhaps an early visit to the cemetery. The least might be daily headaches that you have because you did not work hard, sacrifice yourself (dances, parties, fun, dating), and make proper adjustments according to the needs of your children. Remember, "Pay me now or pay me later." It is definitely your choice. It is definitely the choice of the parent, guardian, relative caregiver, or anyone who is entrusted with the livelihood of a child.

When seeking help for your child, do not be ashamed or hesitant. Do not use unfrequented child advocacy groups, especially the ones not scrutinized by the government. Use city, state, and federal agencies. Use agencies that you are familiar with through word of mouth and not necessarily through television and written advertisements.

Use services that cater to the entire family. If you do, you will receive a more balanced approach to solving problems, and it is also a method of eliminating problems before they occur.

In their formative years, children need an abundance of attention, and they need it constantly. If you do not offer them this attention, they will ultimately obtain it, and I mean from any source available to them.

This attention could be gang attention. It could be sexual attention. (Some parents have a tendency to attempt to protect their girls from premarital sexual episodes, while encouraging the boys to go for it. The boys should also be protected. If parents are of the attitude of protecting the girls and letting the boys sow their oats, then they must realize that the other parents are pushing their boys towards their girls, their family's girls, their friends' girls, the girls in their place of worship, and many other environments. It is wrong on both sides and it should be stopped.) It could be homosexual attention (if you are homophobic). It could be "School is bad" attention. It could be drug attention, and the negative list could go on and on.

On numerous occasions, parents want desperately to be heard when they are confronting one of their children with something that the child did that they are not pleased with. And that is fine. But don't place the focus on yourself to such intensity that you will not listen to your child. All you have to do is shut up and listen (force yourself) and your child will tell you what you want to hear and more. No matter how poorly you get along, you are still best friends, and if you would just listen, you would be surprised at the amount of information you will receive. Oftentimes parents are too busy shouting and yelling. This atmosphere sometimes causes the child to become hostile. And when that happens, you are only going to be told lies, and you will only hear the things they know you want to hear. Be patient and don't worry about how you have experienced the same situations as a child. Your environment could have been wrong. Your parents and guardians could have been wrong in the methods that they used in teaching you, despite the fact that you might have turned out to be a good person. We might not like it, but all people are different and sometimes they have to be taught differently. Do not forget that all parents are parents for the first time, and they are subject to mistakes. However mistakes can be corrected with proper nurturing.

# Section 2
## *Hugs and Kisses*

### A. Say, I Love You
### B. Honesty

    Your child should get meaningful hugs and kisses from birth to death. People need affection and they need it for a lifetime. I do not mean those artificial (name it tradition) hugs and kisses that are performed for the public. In those instances those people involved look around to see who is watching. I mean a real honest hug and kiss, coupled with a legitimate, "I love you." And when you say it, say it looking directly into your child's face. Too often some parents think there is a cutoff point for hugging and kissing and expressing love to their children. That thought is absolutely wrong. This type of affection should last a lifetime.
    There is a family that I know that had a beautiful baby boy. He was so cute. And every day you could see them pouring their love all over him. I was so proud of them I almost burst.
    Oftentimes I could overhear them say, "Oh, he boo booed on himself and his cute clothes got a little dirty. Don't cry baby we will take you inside and clean you up."
    A few years later I was shocked to hear how the mother talked to him. I could tell that the days of hugging, kissing, and saying nice things were definitely over. I overheard her say, "Get your fucking ass off that dirty ass floor, shut up that fucking crying, and go somewhere and get that goddamn shit out of your pants." I could not believe that I heard her say that. I just could not believe my ears. Since that time I have also heard the father say awful things to him. I overheard him say, "Fuck you, nigger, you ain't shit." And I also heard him say some things that I just don't want to repeat. Why did they change towards him? What happened to all of that love, hugs, kisses, and attention that he received in his early years? Today he is serving a life sentence for murder. Am I saying that if they had continued to show him love and affection he

would not be in jail for murder? I honestly believe it is true. I wish it could be put to the test but it can't. However there is one thing that I am sure of, they all paid later.

I was at a friend's house one evening and he was trying to show off in front of me by playing father. I had to leave. His kid was about eight years old and he put on a shirt that his father did not like. His father slapped him hard, "Didn't I tell you not to put on that shirt again?" He yelled at his son as he slapped him harder and harder. "I'm gone kick your ass. I told you never that shirt." He was slapping him so hard and fast the only word of explanation the child could get out was, "But." I thought he was going to kill the kid. I wasn't about to intervene, but I didn't have to sit there and witness that stupidity. So I quietly got up and left. I sat in my truck and as I began to pull away from his house, I heard another slap. The pain that I felt for my friend was enormous. At that moment I knew that his son was hurting, but I also knew my friend was in deep pain, for he was not reacting to the shirt that the boy had on, he was reacting to something quite different and far from his kid, but he was taking it out on his kid.

I didn't know what to do. I was completely lost. I thought about calling the police. I thought about calling the child abuse hot line. I contemplated a few more options, but I did absolutely nothing. Or maybe I did do something; this gentleman could no longer call me his friend.

Please don't do that. Please don't slap them in the face. It is degrading, and it shows a lack of caring. I don't have any problem with spanking on the behind. That fatty tissue can take it as long as you don't become outrageous. Don't slap him and make him mean and non-caring. One day he might kill you, or me.

I witnessed another incident that hurt me dearly. A woman was walking with four small kids. Three appeared to be normal and the fourth one was obviously physically handicapped. The handicapped boy struggled to keep up. At times he would fall and she would look back at him and scream for him to hurry up. He would get up and awkwardly struggle to catch up. She finally slowed down and extended her hand backward so he could catch it for his balance. As soon as he was close enough for him to touch her, she would snatch her hand away and he would grab her back pocket and hold on.

It is so painful to watch something like that. It is the height of man's inhumanity to children. The future for that kid is nonexistent.

Some relative caregivers dwell on the false assumption that if the incident of child abuse is not rape, murder, or kidnapping it is not really child abuse. They are totally wrong.

I hate the thought of abortion, but I'd rather see some kids dead than living the type of lives that I have witnessed throughout my life.

Another very important decision you have to make in parenting is whether or not you are going to be honest. I am not saying that you cannot make a mistake. Making a mistake has nothing to do with honesty, unless you are not strong enough to admit your mistakes.

Create a pact with your children. Throw those contracts and written things away. Don't put it in writing because you want to build as many trust foundations as possible. Never let lies come between you. Let no one interfere with that alliance. And most of all, don't you break it.

Forget the tee shirts and caps with slogans on them, unless they are just for dress. Make your own tee shirt, however crude. Great examples would be, "I love my kids, my daughter is great, my son is great, my kids are staying home." There are many more examples, but you can create your own.

# Section 3
## *Self-Presentation*

### A. Health
### B. Profanity
### C. Firmness
### D. Convictions
### E. Bad Habits

It is very important that your self-presentation is above reproach. You are under a microscope. Your mental, physical, and emotional presentation should be equal to all that you desire from your child (and more) when he or she grows into adulthood. Your cool and total mental state should never have to be questioned by your children. You should have an even temper. I don't mean you should never raise your voice, but when you speak, what you say should only be heard by the ones you are speaking to. Learn to control your temper, and at all costs, learn to and practice distinguishing among correct decision-making values. Don't do anything stupid. However we are all human and realistically we all do ridiculous things occasionally. In that case, admit it, discuss it, and correct it.

Try and keep yourself physically fit: exercise, sports, aerobics. Learn about eating nutritiously. And for heaven's sake avoid the phrase, "One time won't hurt you." Teach your child that a proper diet will have lifelong effects on him or her, and if you are teaching it, practicing it will also be beneficial to your endeavors (discussed thoroughly in chapter six). Avoid obesity and all the other extremes. Don't drink alcoholic beverages (including beer). It is said in many social circles that drinking sociably will not harm you. Social drinking is the only type of drinking that leads to alcoholism. Do not smoke, anything. And for God's sake do not take drugs, and if you already have these bad habits, quit. Please do not use that unpersuasive excuse, "Bad habits are hard to break." Bad habits are broken every day, and you are no less valuable than the other person who gave up a bad habit.

DO NOT USE PROFANITY AROUND YOUR CHILDREN. I repeat, DO NOT USE PROFANITY AROUND YOUR CHILDREN. Do not allow them to associate with people who use profanity (including family members). Absolutely forbid it. If you have the idea that public and loud profanity is fashionable, you will not only have problems with your children, but you will also have problems yourself. Notice the type of people who use profanity. Do you really want your children to be like them? Do you want to be like them? I don't care about the moral changes in society. I don't care about the moral changes in radio and television. And I don't care about changes in the morals of music. But I do care about the children. Separate your children from profanity. Draw the line, set positive examples, let them know that no matter what, you want the best for them.

# Section 4
*Discipline*

A. Religion
B. Failures
C. Teachers
D. Negative Behavior
E. Positive Reinforcement

A major concern in parenting is discipline. In order to change a maladaptive behavior, the first thing you should do is control it. And in order to control it, you must identify it.

Identification of maladjustment in children is not a simple task. It is generally recognized that maladaptive behavior may be expressed by poor academic performance, negative or aggressive behavior, stealing, truancy, and delinquency; however even when overt behavior clues reveal behavior deviation, they do not necessarily reveal the cause and severity of the deviation. Furthermore many children who are emotionally upset do not exhibit these symptoms.

A child may be considered maladjusted when he is so thwarted in satisfaction of his needs for safety, affection, acceptance, and self-esteem that he is unable intellectually to function efficiently, cannot adapt to reasonable requirements of social regulation and convention, or is plagued with inner conflict, anxiety, and guilt, that he is unable to perceive reality clearly or meet the ordinary demands of the environment in which he älives. Symptoms of personal-social maladjustment are not the same for all children. Some are more frequent, however, and some symptoms are more easily observed than others. One student, for example, may be quiet in school, but given to fantasy; another may be aggressive and given to lying, showing off, and quarreling. Some cases of maladjustment can easily be satisfied by the parent. Some cases school and teachers can easily satisfy; others may require a social worker, a clinical psychologist, or a psychiatrist. The symptoms are generally classified into three groups: physical, behavioral, and emotional.

### Physical Signs

| | |
|---|---|
| Facial twitching | Twisting hair |
| Nervous spasms | Restlessness |
| Stuttering | Fidgeting |
| Biting nails | Rapid nervous speech |
| Scratching self | Crying easily |
| Vomiting | Digestive disturbances |
| Enuresis | |

### Behavior Deviations

| | |
|---|---|
| Aggressiveness | Retiring |
| Negativism | Easily embarrassed |
| Night terrors | Sleep disturbed |
| Bullying | Walking in sleep |
| Lying | Masturbation |
| Voluntary mutism | Stubbornness |
| Poor schoolwork | Regression |
| Overly sensitive | |

### Emotional Manifestations

| | |
|---|---|
| Given to worry | Disposition to hate |
| Feelings of inferiority | Resentful |
| Abnormal fears | Temper tantrums |
| Panting | Extreme timidity |

Behavior modification involves changing behavior. All behaviors can be modified if time, patience, and skill are available. Two of the greatest considerations in modifying behavior are strict adherence to individualization and the observation of the behavior to be modified.

One of the most popular methods of behavior modification is positive reinforcement. This author agrees with positive reinforcement, because it is essential to the whole process of behavior modification. Positive reinforcements may include food, money, compliments, hugs, smiles, attention. By no means should you overuse any of these reinforcers.

Negative reinforcers, such as taking away a meal or corporal punishment (spanking), should be avoided. However light spanking is acceptable under certain circumstances.

Be firm but do not be a slave driver. Use tough love. Do not threaten your children. Simply say what you have to say and mean it. If you have to punish them, think about it first and then punish them in a way that you will not have to change later. Do not make a habit of giving in after you have made a decision.

If a man purchases a car, he would demand the manual that goes with the car. This manual will enable him to better understand the car and it will be an aid for proper maintenance. It is the same when it comes to the manual that God, as you understand him, gives us. I recommend religious convictions with your children, but please, it is better not to be religious if you are going to be a phony. Children have this incredible sense of knowing when a parent is phony. That is not the type of relationship you want to build with them.

Listed Below Is a Working List of Suggestions for Parents:
1. Spend time with your children; have fun.
2. When things become tense, use humor to ease them.
3. Look for the good things your children do and praise them for those good things.
4. If the inappropriate behavior can be tolerated, ignore it.
5. Take your children's concerns seriously.
6. Try to be a pleasant person to be around.
7. Encourage your children to talk about their problems.
8. Accept your children's anger.
9. Allow children to do physical things to vent their aggression.
10. Show plenty of affection.
11. Model appropriate behavior.
12. Calmly explain complicated situations.
13. Give rewards for accomplishments and good behavior.
14. Share your positive feelings with your children.
15. Monitor your voice when speaking to them.
16. Use eye to eye contact.
17. Let them know that they come first in your life.
18. Make rules and set limits.
19. Let them know exactly what you expect of them.
20. Love them.

If the Bible says, "Thou shall not steal," there is no room for interpretation. Stealing is stealing. This includes the Sweet n' Low that your child saw you put into your purse or trousers at the restaurant. It includes taking your husband's or wife's last soda and asking the children not to say anything about it. When the mailman goes through the neighborhood and leaves free samples on people's porches and you tell your child to take them for your personal use, that is telling your child to be dishonest. When Jehovah's Witnesses come to the door and you tell your kids to say that you are not at home, these are classic examples of lying, dishonesty, and cowardice.

If you have to lock your refrigerator, you have failed. If your children bring items home that you cannot account for financially, you have failed. If you can't leave money out in plain sight without it disappearing, you have failed. Failure does not mean you should quit. Try again, never stop trying. Perhaps you should change your approach.

Whether you want to be or not, you are the first line of examples for your children.

The saying that "Procrastination is oftentimes beneficial," works well in some instances. However when it comes to your children, do not wait. Do everything humanly possible to enable your children to grow up physically, mentally, morally, emotionally, and spiritually sound.

Beware of the games that money-making people play. Be especially aware of the commercials. "Stay in school" is the worst one. That statement is too isolated. Schools are not made for everyone. I think mandatory education should be abolished. Some children just don't belong in school with our children. I am speaking about the ones who come to school with weapons. Weapons are for fighting and killing, and not for learning. I am speaking of the ones who come to sell drugs. I am speaking of the ones who come to school to fight. I am speaking of the ones who do not receive attention at home and come to school for the sole purpose of disrupting the learning process to gain attention. It is awful and sad for this author to say it, but these types of children can bring your children down to their level and you absolutely do not want that to happen.

Most kids are great, however one disruptive child (one who only cares about drugs, fighting, and extortion) can cause fifteen well-meaning children to miss many days of schooling because of their fear of the disruptive child. Can you imagine what would happen if there were five such disruptive children in one school? People in power are such cowards. They are afraid to make the hard decisions that will eliminate this problem.

Teachers are much the same as mechanics, lawyers, doctors, technicians, and other professionals. They are not cure-alls. They are human and subject to mistakes and failures as others. With that thought in mind, be aware of the teacher who claims that he or she knows the culture simply because they know some of the slang and the handshake.

Do not allow educators to tell you that your child is smarter than he or she actually is. Some educators (teachers, counselors, administrators), for whatever reason, have a tendency to become overzealous with their praise. Frequently they make statements such as, "Your child could be a doctor or lawyer if the effort was put forth." More often than not, those particular children do not have a chance. Know your children well enough to know what they are capable of and guide their educational endeavors accordingly.

Recently (30 June 1993) there were meetings by the powers that be to end or monitor violence on television. They say that television violence causes our children to be violent. NO! NO! NO! If your children are violent, it is your responsibility. You let it happen. These powerful people sit behind these long tables with the bright lights and cameras and argue back and forth while you wait for a decision. Once again you are allowing people you don't know to make decisions for you. You are in fact waiting to relinquish your responsibility to them. As parents you are the leaders of your household. You handle it!

There have been enough meetings and round-table discussions with handpicked kids. Now it is time to bring the parents to meetings and hear from them. Now it is time for the parents to take over. And the first thing they should do is to search the house for all types of weapons. If they find these weapons, they should give them to the police (do not throw them away) and make no excuses. They should also encourage their friends and neighbors to do the same thing. As a matter of fact, there should be a nationwide attempt for parents to disarm their children.

Parents should inform their children that it is not enough for a rich man, a television star, or a popular athlete to appear on television and make the statement, "Stay in school." That is absolutely not saying enough. A better statement may be, "If your goal is to learn and to learn only, stay in school." "Say no to drugs" is another saying that has made someone millions. "Say no to drugs" is a request for a verbal commitment. It is not a request for a physical, mental, or emotional commitment. Parents should make themselves the drug of choice. And when their children need an uplift, they should feel comfortable in coming to them for that emotional uplift. The greatest high in the world is the high that comes from parental praise.

Schools visited by people who are already rich are a joke. Children should hear from people who are struggling. It should be people who have just pulled themselves up by their bootstraps. It should be people who have not quite made it. It should be people in jail (or on their way), especially those in jail for life. It should be street people. At least there should be a balance between those who are almost there and those who are still struggling. Let the schools know your feelings. This is a suggestion for you to become totally absorbed in your children's education.

Keep life simple. Do not financially endanger yourself by purchasing something that you cannot afford. Do not take trips that you cannot afford. Ignore unaffordable fashions and teach your children to admire nice things, but also teach them not to become fashion maniacs.

Most teachings have to be accomplished in the children's early years. You simply cannot wait until your children are teenagers to begin teaching them. For example if your daughter plays outside with the other children and you allow her to come inside when she gets ready because she is not of the age and build to be sexually attractive, but as soon as her hips and breasts begin to develop, you then decide that she can no longer go outside or come in at will, forget it. You cannot stop her without serious problems.

# Section 5
## *Sports*

Sports do not stop crime. No matter who says they do, they are wrong. SPORTS DO NOT STOP CRIME.

Athletes should show their support for schools, non-drug addiction, and nonviolence on their different playing surfaces and communities. This could easily be accomplished by them if they would stop fighting, cursing, complaining, and a host of other things that they do on their courts and in their environments. However by doing these right things, they do not become role models. That is forever a parental caregiver's job, but they do, however, become examples (selected).

It is applaudable for some community leaders to discuss playgrounds, recreation centers, and baseball teams as methods to combat crime. It was tried in the sixties but it did not work. It was tried in the seventies and it did not work, and it is not going to work in the nineties.

These sports and recreation activities do not reach the people who they were designed to reach.

Parenting is the answer. Back to basics is the solution. Nurturing is the key.

# Section 6
## *Nutrition*

There is increasing recognition among parents, doctors, and diet specialists that nutrition plays an important role in the stability of a child's life. They feel that diet and nutrition have a great deal to do with the educational endeavors and emotional stability of the child.

When children suffer from chronic undernourishment, evidence of physiological and biochemical changes in the central nervous system is evident. Inadequate nutrient intake affects the development of the brain during the period of rapid growth. This period of rapid growth occurs during the last three months of pregnancy and the first six months of infancy. During the first three years of life, 90% of the total growth of the brain takes place (H.V. Kelly, 1983).

Nutrient deficiencies produce certain deficiency symptoms. One example is a deficiency of thiamine (vitamin $B_1$) which may produce irritability, nervousness, and even increased sensitivity to noise. Sometimes a teacher observes that a child is not meeting his potential (not motivated). This is often a clue to the presence of an iron deficiency.

Under-nutrition definitely affects performance in an adverse manner. It is not an easy task to measure these effects. Lack of energy and difficulty in concentration may create long-term problems. Poor nutrition not only has an effect on the central nervous system, but it also may result in severe learning disabilities which may lead to poor interactions with other people and the environment. This could result in a vicious cycle. The kind of food and the amount of food we eat matter.

Despite the fact that research (1994) funded by the sugar industry indicates that sugar is not harmful to the body in the areas of hyperactivity and learning disorders, this author believes that the information is not totally true. Sugar is one of the most substantial nutritional problems. Foods high in concentrated sweets (refined sugar, sodas, jellies, fruit punches, flavored gelatin, cookies) are low in essential nutrients. Sugar is classed as the culprit in producing symptoms of hyperactivity and learning disorders. Artificial colors and artificial flavors are hyperactive and learning disability culprits.

There are quite a few foods that I recommend that parents avoid or limit. It may be shocking but true. It is extremely important to develop good eating habits. Not only will developing wholesome eating habits benefit children at present, but it will also develop wholesome attitudes and habits for later life.

Certain meats and fish should be avoided: marbled beef, pork, bacon, sausage, and other pork products; fatty fowl (duck, goose); skin and fat of turkey and chicken; processed meats; luncheon meats (salami, bologna); frankfurters and fast food hamburgers (they are loaded with fat); organ meats (kidney, liver); and canned fish packed in oil.

Avoid avocados. Starchy vegetables (potatoes, corn, lima beans, dried peas, beans) may be used only if substitutes for a serving of bread or cereal.

Limit your intake of baked goods with shortening and/or sugar. Commercial mixes with dried eggs and whole milk should be avoided. Also avoid sweetened packaged cereals (sugar-covered cereals). The added sugar converts into triglycerides.

Butter, lard, and all fats, bacon drippings, gravies, cream sauces, as well as palm and coconut oils, should be eliminated from your diet. All of these are high in saturated fats. Examine labels on cholesterol-free products for hydrogenated fats (these are oils that have been hardened into solids and in the process have became saturated).

Later in a child's life he or she will, for health reasons, have to stop eating certain foods. It may be a good policy to limit some of these foods in their early years so it will not be extremely difficult to stop later. Some of these foods are cakes, cookies, candy, ice cream (junk food), and also sugar fruit juices and soft drinks, cocoa made with whole milk and/or sugar, potato chips, chocolate, jams, jellies, syrups, whole milk puddings, milk sherbet, and hydrogenated peanut butter, and all of these should be of major concern. Do not let the grandparents win attention favors by giving your children junk food. Alcohol of any type should be avoided.

It is recommended that children do not eat certain foods, and by the same token, wholesome foods should be recommended. Some meats to choose are lean meats such as chicken, turkey, veal, and nonfat cuts of beef with the excess fat and skin removed. Also recommended are fresh or frozen fish, canned fish packed in water, and shellfish such as lobster, crabs, shrimp, and oysters. However these shellfish should be limited to one serving per week. Shellfish are high in cholesterol but low in saturated fat. The meats and fish that were mentioned should be broiled or baked on a rack. Egg substitutes and egg whites can be used freely.

Three servings of fresh fruit should be consumed per day. At least one citrus fruit should be eaten daily. Frozen or canned fruit with no sugar or syrup may be eaten.

There is no limit as to how many vegetables can be eaten. One dark green or one deep yellow vegetable is recommended daily. Cauliflower, broccoli, and celery, as well as potato skins, are recommended for fiber. It is preferable to steam vegetables, but they may be boiled, strained, or braised with polyunsaturated vegetable oil.

I recommend 1/2 cup of hot cereal or 3/4 cup of cold cereal per day. Add a sugar substitute if desired, with fat-free or skim milk.

Dessert snacks should be limited to two servings per day. Substitute each serving for a bread/cereal serving: ice milk, water sherbet; unflavored gelatin or gelatin flavored with sugar substitutes; pudding prepared with skim milk; egg white souffles; unbuttered popcorn. I recommend such beverages as fresh fruit juices, soft drinks with sugar substitutes, club soda, cocoa made with skim milk or nonfat dried milk and water, clear broth, and spring water.

## EXCLUDE THESE FAST FOODS
(Contents: additives, preservatives, dyes, sugar, etc.)

| Item | Calories | Carbo-hydrates (g) | Fats (g) | Sodium (mg) |
|---|---|---|---|---|
| McDonald's Big Mac | 541 | 39 | 31 | 962 |
| Burger King Whopper | 606 | 51 | 32 | 909 |
| Burger Chef hamburger | 258 | 24 | 13 | 393 |
| Dairy Queen cheese dog | 330 | 24 | 19 | NA |
| Taco Bell taco | 186 | 14 | 8 | 79 |
| Arthur Treacher's fish (sa) | 440 | 68 | 18 | 836 |
| Burger King Whaler | 486 | 64 | 46 | 735 |
| McDonald's Filet-O-Fish | 402 | 34 | 23 | 709 |
| Long John Silver (fish-2-p) | 318 | 19 | 19 | NA |
| McDonald's Egg McMuffin | 352 | 26 | 20 | 914 |
| Burger King french fries | 214 | 28 | 10 | 05 |
| Arthur Treacher's cole slaw | 123 | 11 | 8 | 266 |
| Dairy Queen onion rings | 300 | 33 | 17 | NA |
| McDonald's apple pie | 300 | 31 | 19 | 414 |
| Burger King vanilla shake | 332 | 50 | 11 | 159 |
| McDonald's chocolate shake | 364 | 60 | 9 | 329 |
| Dairy Queen banana split | 540 | 91 | 15 | NA |

## AVOID OR LIMIT THESE ITEMS WITH HIDDEN GRANULATED SUGAR CONTENT

| Food Item | Portion | Gran. Sugar (tsps.) |
|---|---|---|
| Chocolate cake | 1 | 6 |
| Cupcake | 1 | 6 |
| Donut (glazed) | 1 | 6 |
| Soft drinks | 1 | 6 |
| Chocolate milk | 1 | 6 |
| Apple pie | 1 slice | 7 |
| Malted milk shake | 10 oz. glass | 5 |
| Angel food cake | 1-4 oz. piece | 7 |
| Chocolate cake, iced | 1 slice | 10 |
| Cupcake, iced | 1-4 oz. piece | 6 |
| Fig Newtons | 1 | 5 |
| Macaroons | 1 | 6 |
| Sugar cookies | 1 | 7 |
| Hard candy | 4 oz. | 20 |
| Ice cream sundae | 1 | 7 |
| Ice cream bar | 1 | 1-7 |
| Cocoa malt | 1 glass | 6 |
| White icing | 1 oz. | 5 |
| Jelly | 1 tsp. | 4-6 |
| Orange marmalade | 1 tsp. | 4-6 |
| Strawberry jam | 1 tsp. | 4-6 |
| Berry pie | 1 slice | 10 |
| Cherry pie | 1 slice | 10 |
| Lemon pie | 1 slice | 7 |
| Pecan pie | 1 slice | 7 |
| Date pudding | 1/2 cup | 7 |
| Fig pudding | 1/2 cup | 7 |
| Berry tart | 1 cup | 10 |
| Sherbet | 1/2 cup | 9 |

Please note that the sugar listed here represents the granulated sugars placed inside of these products, and it does not represent all the other types of sugars within these items.

## BREAKFAST CEREALS NOT RECOMMENDED
### (SUGAR IN BREAKFAST CEREALS)

| Product | Total Sugar (%) | Sucrose |
|---|---|---|
| Alpha Bits | 38 | 38 |
| Apple Jacks | 54.6 | |
| Cap'n Crunch | 40 | 40 |
| Cap'n Crunch Crunch Berries | 43.3 | 42 |
| Cap'n Crunch Peanut Butter | 32.2 | 31 |
| Cocoa Krispies | 43 | 41 |
| Cocoa Pebbles | 42.6 | 42 |
| Cocoa Puffs | 33.3 | 32 |
| Cookie Crisp, Chocolate | 41 | 40 |
| Cookie Crisp, Oatmeal | 40.1 | 38 |
| Cookie Crisp, Vanilla | 43.5 | 43 |
| Corny Snaps | 45.5 | 45 |
| Count Chocula | 39.5 | 35 |
| Country Crisp | 22 | 18 |
| Craklin' Bran | 29 | 27 |
| Crazy Cow Chocolate | 45.6 | 42 |
| Crazy Cow, Strawberry | 40.1 | 38 |
| Frankenberry | 43.7 | 38 |
| Froot Loops | 48 | 48 |
| Frosted Mini Wheats | 26 | 26 |
| Frosted Rice | 37 | 35 |
| Frosted Rice Krinkles | 44 | 43.3 |
| Fruity Pebbles | 42.4 | 42 |
| Golden Grahams | 30 | 27 |
| Honey Comb | 37.2 | 37 |
| Lucky Charms | 42.2 | 36 |
| C.W. Post | 28.7 | 20 |
| C.W. Post Raisin | 29 | 18 |
| Quisp | 40.7 | 40 |
| Raisin Bran, Kellogg's | 29 | 11 |
| Sugar Corn Pops | 46 | 39 |
| Sugar Frosted Flakes of Corn | 41 | 39 |
| Sugar Smacks | 56 | 43 |
| Sugar Super Crisp | 46 | 36 |
| Trix | 35.9 | 33 |

I totally disagree with the statement that hungry children cannot learn. They can learn, however they will be learning under trying conditions.

Children should eat the types of foods that enable them to live a life free of education disruptions and illness. It is the responsibility of parents, shared with teachers and school administrators, to ascertain that children are provided with, or familiarized with, diets free of large amounts of additives, sugars, and preservatives.

First, parents should provide, at a very early age, the types of balanced meals necessary to develop wholesome eating habits. It is this author's belief that if children begin life with wholesome attitudes towards the foods that they ingest (not to fill the stomach but to nourish the body), it is possible that these attitudes will continue through later life. Parents should prepare a wholesome breakfast (chart enclosed) for their children before school. If it is not available at home, most schools provide a free breakfast for their students (if the child is of school age). Hopefully, with guidance, the child will not stop at the store to buy gum, candy, soda, and cookies for breakfast.

Second, teachers should teach, across the curriculum, vitamin and nutritional values (chart enclosed) and provide exemplary examples by using the lunch that they bring to school and lunch they eat in the teachers' lunchroom. Teachers should teach from kindergarten through twelfth grade the health, social, and emotional problems resulting from improper eating habits. Health problems may include lack of energy, obesity, diseased and decayed teeth. Social problems may follow health problems by encompassing obesity and decayed teeth. Embarrassment, teasing, and ridicule may cause emotional problems.

Third, for the most part, school administrators do plan well-balanced meals for their school systems, but they do not adhere to strict policy enforcement of these plans. Schools usually succumb to the wishes of the student body and provide large amounts of junk food. These foods may include candy, potato chips, soda, gum, and other goodies. School administrators should continue to provide well-balanced meals for their school systems, but they should be more diligent in enforcing proper nutritional policies. Oftentimes school administrators allow certain clubs and special interest groups (Brownies, scouts, home, and school) to sell their junk food in school. These foods are not recommended for our children for consumption on a daily basis. They also, at times, allow vending machines full of junk food to be installed in the schools. All junk food should be eliminated from all school systems.

As I indicated earlier, I do believe that a hungry child can learn. However I firmly believe the research that indicates that children who eat well-balanced meals in adequate amounts perform better in the classroom, in the areas of attention, work completion, not being disruptive, and positive attitudes towards learning, compared to students who do not eat well-balanced meals in adequate amounts.

Parents, teachers, administrators, and nutrition experts should jointly engage in seminars, workshops, and in-service education to study this problem and to share solutions to the problem. At times each official or parent thinks the other one is engaged in nutrition education and at times neither is engaged in it. This issue is so important that each person (parent, teacher, administrator, and nutrition expert) should know what the other person is doing to ascertain that someone is doing what is right for the children.

If my recommendations are not possible to follow, parents should take the initiative to investigate the proper nutrition for their children. They should respond to their findings according to their financial capabilities.

Parents should not attempt to bribe their children with junk food.

## Nutrition Programs Recommended

Major nutrition programs are essential for the health, welfare, and education of school children. Each year the Pennsylvania Department of Education provides a Nutrition Education and Training (NET) program for food service providers, teachers, and administrators. NET has been funded by the U.S. Department of Agriculture since 1978.

The program's main purpose is to increase the nutritional knowledge of administrators, teachers, food service personnel, and children in schools and child care institutions in Pennsylvania. It is viewed as a way to gain a better understanding of the relationship between nutritional status and academic performance of children (*Inside Education*, 1991).

The program has numerous goals. They are:
- to encourage students to incorporate nutrition knowledge, health education, and physical fitness into their life styles;
- to increase the nutritional knowledge of preschool children in child care institutions;
- to increase awareness of school administrators, teachers, and food service personnel of the advantages of a comprehensive child nutrition program;
- to increase nutrition education among students in grades 5 to 9;
- to enable schools to measure students' nutrition knowledge.

The effects of good nutrition on a student's ability to learn have been documented in small ways for a number of years. Most classroom teachers recognize which students have had breakfast or lunch by the activity level, comprehension, and attention span of the children in the classroom.

In a recent issue of *Nutrition News* (Fall 1989), Dr. Alan Meyers cites a recent study by researchers at Boston and Tufts universities on whether the beneficial effect on the cognitive performance of grade school children reported by others might be occurring in schools offering the School Breakfast Program (SBP), (*Inside Education*, 1991).

Meyers is a pediatrician in the Division of Ambulatory Pediatrics at Boston City Hospital and an assistant professor of pediatrics at Boston University School of Medicine. He has a special interest in the public health aspects of pediatric nutrition and is working with colleagues to develop a screening system to identify and follow children with moderate to severe under-nutrition.

According to *Inside Education*, the researchers examined the records of over 1,000 third to sixth graders in the Lawrence, Massachusetts public schools. An SBP had just been initiated there under a state mandate requiring all "severe need" schools to begin the program. Controlling for other variables, Meyers and his group found that participation in the program was associated with a statistically significant increase in achievement test scores (Comprehensive Tests of Basic Skills) and improvements in tardiness and absentee rates (*Inside Education*, 1991).

While these results await confirmation by other investigators, the Pennsylvania Department of Education has comparable results from questions asked with the March 1990 TELLS program.

Eight questions about student eating habits were included in the questionnaire given to all third, fifth, and eighth graders taking the test. The results showed that 69.9% of the third graders, 59.4% of the fifth graders, and 37.9% of the eighth graders ate breakfast every day (some indication that daily eating habit declines with age).

Preliminary data compares the math and reading scores students received about their eating habits. In all cases, test scores were three to five points higher for those students who ate breakfast at least five days a week than those who did not eat breakfast at all.

Over half the students who ate breakfast the morning of the test selected milk and bread for breakfast. When the students were asked where they ate that morning, 78% ate at home and 4% ate at school (*Inside Education*, 1991).

A child's nutritional status and its future impact begin with pregnancy, but all of them are interwoven with the impact of nutrition.

Low birth weight, which is one of the most important indicators of whether newborn babies will grow and develop normally, is related to a mother's nutritional status before and during her pregnancy. Babies with low birth weights run a greater risk of being mentally retarded or of suffering visual and hearing impairments. They are also more likely to have behavior and learning problems in later life.

Recent research confirms the links between poor nutrition during pregnancy and children's behavioral and learning ability:

> School age children in San Diego, California, whose mothers were undernourished during pregnancy, interacted less with their peers, were more dependent on adults, and were sadder and more unfriendly. The national evaluation of the special supplemental food program for women, infants, and children, a federal program that provides nutritious foods to low-income pregnant women, new mothers, and young children at nutritional risk, showed that participation in the program decreased low birth weight rates and improved children's intellectual ability.

Considering the high rate of teen pregnancy in the U.S., the nutritional status of adolescents is of particular concern. If adolescents do not have good nutrition habits before they become pregnant, it will be difficult for them to catch up once pregnancy has started. Unfortunately many studies have shown teens to be the poorly nourished Americans who tend to have the lowest participation rates in the school meals program (*Inside Education*, 1991).

Another early influence on children's nutritional status is the adequacy of foods consumed while children are in day care. If preschoolers in day care do not get enough food or the right kinds of food, they will be at risk of hunger and under-nutrition.

Survey results from around the country indicate that a significant number of children are suffering from hunger and/or under-nutrition. National studies confirm the existence of these problems. According to the U.S. Public Health Service, one of the surgeon general's 1990 health objectives for the nation was eliminating growth retardation of infants and children caused by inadequate diets.

The impact of mild under-nutrition cannot be easily measured except for eventual growth retardation. However it can have serious effects:

1. Under-nutrition increases the risk of illness and its severity;
2. Under-nutrition has a negative effect on children's ability to learn. It is difficult to isolate and measure the effects of chronic under-nutrition because many other aspects of poverty may negatively affect a child's development. However the consensus of researchers in this area is that under-nutrition does have an independent effect on learning behavior;
3. The learning-related effects of under-nutrition start happening before any visible signs of growth retardation occur. Undernourished children are less physically active, less attentive, and less independent and curious. They are more anxious and less responsive socially, and they cannot concentrate as well. As a result,

their reading ability, verbal skills, and motor skills suffer. These effects do not have to be permanent if better nutrition is provided and the environment improves;
4. Iron deficiency anemia is a specific kind of under-nutrition and is one of the most prevalent nutritional problems in the U.S., especially among young children. Even mild cases lead to shortened attention span, irritability, fatigue, and decreased ability to concentrate. Anemic children do poorly on vocabulary, reading, mathematics, problem-solving, and psychological tests (*Inside Education*, 1991).

## Some Food Recommended for Consumption
Satisfy the Sweet Tooth Nutritionally

Instead of a soft drink, you can drink a juice spritzer. Mix equal parts of fruit juice and club soda or seltzer water—for extra zip, add slices of lemon, lime, and orange.

Instead of Jello, mix three envelopes of unflavored gelatin and 1/2 cup of cold water. Heat 1-1/2 cups unsweetened fruit juice (examples: grape, orange, pineapple).

Instead of fruited yogurt, eat plain or vanilla low-fat yogurt with your own fresh fruit added. Try adding a little vanilla extract or cinnamon, too.

Instead of candy, introduce children to dried fruits like raisins, banana chips, prunes, apricots, and frozen grapes. Fresh fruits are also recommended: grapes, cantaloupe, watermelon, oranges, apples, pears, bananas, etc. These fresh fruits can be eaten as they are or parents, nutritionists, school administrators, and students can use their imaginations and prepare these fruits in a variety of ways: fruit salads, animal fruit, etc.

Instead of instant cocoa, a delicious drink could be obtained by mixing 1 heaping teaspoon of unsweetened cocoa, 2 teaspoons of a sugar substitute, 2 teaspoons of cold milk, and add 1 cup of hot milk or hot water, and stir well and serve.

Instead of sweetened instant oatmeal, add raisins, cinnamon, allspice, and milk to regular or unsweetened instant oatmeal; also make your own instant oatmeal by chopping regular oatmeal in a blender and then adding boiling water.

Instead of fruit flavored punch or drink, drink 100% fruit juices such as orange, apple, or grape. Drink water liberally.

As breakfast food, this author recommends cereal such as Rice Chex, Corn Chex, and Wheat Chex. This author highly recommends Shredded Wheat by Nabisco, Puffed Wheat by Quaker, and Puffed Rice by Quaker (Penn. State Nutrition Center).

## MINERALS

| Nutrient | Functions | Sources | Deficiencies |
|---|---|---|---|
| Calcium | • Strengthens teeth and bones<br>• Helps blood clot<br>• Helps muscles contract and relax<br>• Helps nerves send signals | • Milk, yogurt, cheese, collards, kale, turnip, and mustard greens | • Rickets (bowed legs)<br>• Osteoporosis (thin bones) |
| Iron | • Helps body use energy<br>• Forms part of red blood cells | • Prune juice, liver, dried beans, peas, red meat | • Fatigue<br>• Anemia<br>• Poor concentration |
| Magnesium | • Helps fight depression<br>• Helps prevent heart attack<br>• Promotes healthy teeth and bones | • Grapefruit, lemons, nuts, seeds, apples, dark green vegetables | • Nervousness<br>• Depression<br>• Unable to sleep<br>• Sensitive to noise<br>• Nerve and muscle damage |
| Phosphorus | • Promotes growth and repair of cells<br>• Helps use starches<br>• Promotes healthy gums and teeth | • Eggs, nuts, fish, poultry, meat, whole grains | • Rickets (bowed legs) |
| Potassium | • Reduces blood pressure<br>• Sends oxygen to brain to think clearly<br>• Helps in waste removal | • Orange juice, citrus fruits, green leafy vegetables, bananas | • Low blood sugar<br>• Edema (retaining water)<br>• Abnormal heartbeat<br>• Muscle weakness |
| Chlorine | • Keeps you limber<br>• Helps with digestion | • Table salt, kelp, olives | • Loss of teeth and hair |
| Sodium | • Prevents heat exhaustion<br>• Aids in proper nerve and muscle function | • Salt, shellfish, kidney, bacon, carrots, beets, table salt | • Difficulty in digestion of carbohydrates<br>• Muscle weakness |

## VITAMINS

| Nutrient | Functions | Sources | Deficiencies |
|---|---|---|---|
| A<br>Retinol | • Helps skin form mucous membranes<br>• Used in night vision | • Carrots, sweet potatoes, yams, green leafy vegetables | • Dry mucous membranes<br>• Night blindness |
| C<br>Ascorbic Acid | • Forms a substance that holds cells together<br>• Strengthens blood vessels, helps resist infection | • Broccoli, oranges, grapefruit, tomatoes, strawberries | • Frequent bruising<br>• Loose teeth<br>• Gum disease |
| $B_1$<br>Thiamine | • Helps body use carbohydrates<br>• Promotes healthy nervous system | • Lean pork, nuts, fortified cereal, peas, beans, rice, pasta | • Muscle weakness, leg cramps, mental confusion |
| $B_2$<br>Riboflavin | • Helps release energy from foods<br>• Promotes appetite<br>• Helps nervous system | • Liver, milk, yogurt, cottage cheese | • Vision problems<br>• Skin problems<br>• Sore red tongue |
| $B_3$<br>Niacin | • Helps body use energy<br>• Promotes healthy skin and nerves | • Liver, meat, poultry, fish, peanuts, fortified cereal | • Abnormal liver function<br>• High blood sugar |
| $B_6$<br>Pyrodoxine | • Helps body absorb protein<br>• Helps body use fats<br>• Helps form blood cells | • Whole grain cereals, red meats, liver, legumes | • Poor growth<br>• Anemia<br>• Convulsions<br>• Kidney, liver, skin damage |
| $B_{12}$<br>Cobalamin | • Helps form red blood cells<br>• Helps nervous system | • Liver, kidney, meat, fish, eggs, milk, oysters | • Anemia<br>• Nerve damage |
| D<br>Calciferol | • Helps use calcium and phosphorus for healthy bones and teeth | • Fortified dairy products, fish liver oils, egg yolk, salmon | • Rickets (bowed legs)<br>• Poor teeth<br>• Soft bones |

# Section 7
## *Fighting*

### A. Schematic Design
### B. Research

Section Seven is an extremely difficult section. Fighting in the African American community is at epidemic proportions. Females are beginning to fight more and more, and it is becoming more prevalent. However at the moment I want to address the fighting posture of the males.

Fighting has been an institution for African males since early history. Early African tribes (West Africa) fought for territorial rights, food supply, and they also fought for the attainment of their mates. Mimic fighting began for young African males at a very early age. This type of behavior was exhibited to ascertain that when the young men grew up, they would be ready for real tribal warfare.

As time elapsed, the types of fighting and weapons used changed drastically. The early transition of weapons was from sticks and stones to spears and bows and arrows. Killings went from social encounter to a total cultural upheaval. Fight mimicking by the young prospective tribal warriors went from noncontact activities to bloodletting and physical continuum after practice. This fighting ethos was in the African community.

During the slave trade, Africans were thoroughly disseminated. Throughout the world Africans fought in wars large and small. In the case of wars, fighting is expected. As a matter of fact soldiers are killers.

Social fighting has prevailed and will continue until the end of time. However African Americans have taken social fighting from the ridiculous to doltish insensate. As I mentioned earlier, social fighting is at epidemic proportions in some African American communities. It is commonplace to see or hear fistfights, shootings, or knifings daily. These fights sometimes stem from a stolen mate, stolen money, or sometimes a trivial stare. Fistfights are super-epidemic. It is common to see small children, young adults, and old people fighting. And they can be seen everywhere: streets, homes, churches, recreation areas, sporting events, and schools (including colleges and universities).

Fighting is extremely disruptive to the learning process. The disruption that follows a fight or an impending fight is enormous. As soon as the indication of a fight is evident, learning ceases to exist in the classroom. The conversation diverts to possible outcomes of the fight, the joy of seeing the fight, and which one of the participants is the "punk." If two perpetrators seem to want to forget the fight, there are those who will not let that happen. Those persons are called instigators. They will lie, probe, or do anything to keep the fight fires burning.

If the classroom teacher is not prepared for the fighting attitude of the African American, he or she is going to have a very long day.

Parents must band together to stop this sickness, and it is a sickness. Young men fight because someone looks at them, because "he ain't no punk," he stepped on my toe, he touched me when he passed by, he didn't respect me, he stood too close, and numerous other things that are quite infinitesimal.

When these young men witness a fight, there are visible signs of joy. They grab their crotches with gleeful smiles on their faces. They lick their lips and urge the fight on. In some instances they develop an erection while viewing a fight. IT IS A SICKNESS. This is a severe problem and it needs to be addressed.

It is a sorrowful state when a large part of the male population of a race of people has as its forte the ability to fight. When there is a fight, everyone loses. It is also sorrowful when, in the African American early years, more emphasis is placed on how to make a fist and swing than the study of phonetics and diacritical markings. And to gain sexual gratification from fighting or viewing a fight is total sickness.

This author believes that it is possible that African American young men ALSO fight because that is their only method of self-expression. As they are growing up, for numerous reasons they are not allowed to express themselves verbally. They are constantly being told to sit down, be quiet, and shut up by non-caring or non-understanding parents and relatives. Therefore they sometimes express themselves to their peers, for their peers and others in their environment, by way of the fight.

I have not begun to scratch the surface of the reasons of and the solution to the fighting attitude of the African American male. I am merely hoping some of these ideas will stir the emotions of parents, guardians, and relative caregivers. And hopefully people who are more eminently qualified than I will follow my futile attempt by developing some ideas that will slow this heinous attitude.

Parents, quite a few women are working, or have you noticed? The men are standing in welfare lines, hanging around bars all day, or lying around in the morgue. TAKE THEIR WEAPONS, NOW! Hold your children in your arms and tell them that you love them. Please do not use the everyday sayings on caps and tee shirts (I am somebody). Say things from your heart and mean them. If they reject it, it's only because you have waited too long. Do it again and again and again, and soon they will accept it. It takes a beginning. This is a beginning for you.

## Research

Research was compiled on 202 students. These students were classified as having maladaptive behaviors. Their ages ranged from eight to nineteen. They are of low socioeconomic status, and they are all African Americans. Usually the author of the study analyzes the data that is compiled, however this time, I want the parents and other interested parties to study the data and analyze it and ask themselves the following questions:
1. What does this information mean? and
2. What can I do about it?
   (a) If nothing, why?
   (b) If something, what?

## Table 1
## Family Background (Actual Number) 1/y

| Grade | Number of Students | One Parent | Mother Only | Father Only | Grandparents | Others* |
|---|---|---|---|---|---|---|
| 7 | 36 | 30 | 20 | 2 | 12 | 2 |
| 8 | 45 | 39 | 37 | 0 | 2 | 6 |
| 9 | 68 | 51 | 50 | 1 | 10 | 7 |
| 10 | 32 | 32 | 30 | 0 | 2 | 0 |
| 11 | 13 | 9 | 7 | 1 | 4 | 1 |
| 12 | 8 | 8 | 1 | 1 | 0 | 6 |

Key
1. Live with Friend (peer)
2. Live with Friend (mate)
3. Live with Relative (other than listed)
4. Live Alone
5. Live in Foster Home
1/y = Half Year (Sept.-Jan.)

*Others

## Table 2
### Academic Performance
### (Grade Average by Class) 1/y

| Grade | Number of Students | English | Science | Math | History | Health | Physical Education |
|-------|-------------------|---------|---------|------|---------|--------|--------------------|
| 7  | 36 | C | C | D | D | B | B |
| 8  | 45 | C | C | D | D | B | B |
| 9  | 68 | F | F | F | F | C | C |
| 10 | 32 | D | D | D | D | B | B |
| 11 | 13 | D | D | D | D | B | B |
| 12 | 8  | C | C | C | C | B | A |

*Key*
A = 90-100
B = 80-89
C = 70-79
D = 65-69
F = 0-64
1/y = Half Year (Sept.-Jan.)

## Table 3
## Sensations Felt from Fighting
### (Based on Class Percentage 100%) 1/y

| Grade | Number of Students | Happy | Sad | Happy and Sad | No Feeling |
|-------|-------------------|-------|-----|---------------|------------|
| 7     | 36                | 0     | 0   | 100           | 0          |
| 8     | 45                | 60    | 0   | 40            | 0          |
| 9     | 68                | 95    | 0   | 5             | 0          |
| 10    | 32                | 50    | 0   | 50            | 0          |
| 11    | 13                | 0     | 0   | 15            | 85         |
| 12    | 8                 | 0     | 0   | 10            | 90         |

*Key*
1/y = Half Year (Sept.-Jan.)

## Table 4
## Incidence of Classroom Fights by Class Subjects Based on Half of a Year (Sept.-Jan.) 1/y

| Grade | Number of Students | Hygiene | Physical Education | Music | Science | History |
|---|---|---|---|---|---|---|
| 7 | 36 | 0 | 0 | 1 | 2 | 3 |
| 8 | 45 | 0 | 0 | 1 | 0 | 3 |
| 9 | 68 | 1 | 2 | 2 | 3 | 3 |
| 10 | 32 | 0 | 0 | 1 | 1 | 1 |
| 11 | 13 | 1 | 0 | 0 | 1 | 2 |
| 12 | 8 | 0 | 0 | 0 | 2 | 2 |

*Key*
1/y = Half Year (Sept.-Jan.)

## Table 5
## Categories of Fights
### (Average and Locations) 1/y

| Grade | Number of Students | Average Age | Average Daily Fight | Minor Fight | Major Fight | Home Fight | School Fight | Status |
|-------|-------------------|-------------|---------------------|-------------|-------------|------------|--------------|--------|
| 7  | 36 | 13 | 11 | 11 | 0 | 3 | 4 | Low |
| 8  | 45 | 14 | 12 | 10 | 0 | 3 | 4 | Low |
| 9  | 68 | 16 | 20 | 15 | 5 | 6 | 8 | Low |
| 10 | 32 | 17 | 6  | 5  | 3 | 1 | 1 | Low |
| 11 | 13 | 18 | 5  | 2  | 1 | 0 | 1 | Low |
| 12 | 8  | 18 | 2  | 1  | 1 | 0 | 1 | Low |

*Key*
1/y = Half Year (Sept.-Jan.)
Major Fight—Bloodletting, possible weapon, hospitalization necessary
Minor Fight—Short duration, no harm, no disciplinary action necessary

## Table 6
## Students Who Respect Teachers
## (Male and Female Teachers) 1/y

| Grade | Number of Students | English | | Science | | Math | | History | | Homeroom Teacher | | Health | | Physical Education | |
|---|---|---|---|---|---|---|---|---|---|---|---|---|---|---|---|
| | | M | F | M | F | M | F | M | F | M | F | M | F | M | F |
| 7 | 36 | 35 | 1 | 30 | 6 | 32 | 3 | 30 | 6 | 28 | 7 | 36 | 36 | 36 | 36 |
| 8 | 45 | 30 | 0 | 3 | 0 | 10 | 0 | 20 | 2 | 44 | 1 | 39 | 10 | 40 | 6 |
| 9 | 68 | 10 | 0 | 18 | 2 | 50 | 1 | 26 | 4 | 59 | 9 | 50 | 6 | 60 | 10 |
| 10 | 32 | 11 | 0 | 12 | 1 | 10 | 4 | 19 | 6 | 20 | 1 | 30 | 5 | 32 | 12 |
| 11 | 13 | 10 | 5 | 9 | 7 | 11 | 6 | 6 | 11 | 13 | 0 | 12 | 10 | 12 | 19 |
| 12 | 8 | 8 | 8 | 8 | 8 | 8 | 8 | 8 | 8 | 8 | 8 | 8 | 8 | 8 | 8 |

*Key*
0 = No Female Teachers
1/y = Half Year (Sept.-Jan.)

## Table 7
## Attendance Record
## (by Day of the Week)
## Average Number Per Class Absent 1/y

| Grade | Number of Students | Monday | Tuesday | Wednesday | Thursday | Friday |
|---|---|---|---|---|---|---|
| 7 | 36 | 10 | 5 | 3 | 3 | 10 |
| 8 | 45 | 8 | 4 | 4 | 4 | 9 |
| 9 | 68 | 20 | 3 | 6 | 5 | 25 |
| 10 | 32 | 5 | 2 | 2 | 2 | 8 |
| 11 | 13 | 5 | 5 | 5 | 1 | 6 |
| 12 | 8 | 2 | 1 | 0 | 0 | 1 |

*Key*
1/y = Half Year (Sept.–Jan.)

## Table 8
### Average Fight Opponent
### Based on 1/y (Percentage)

| Grade | Number of Students | Males | Females | Teachers | Peers | Parents | Siblings | Others |
|---|---|---|---|---|---|---|---|---|
| 7 | 36 | 49 | 50 | 0 | 100 | 0 | 1 | 0 |
| 8 | 45 | 79 | 20 | 0 | 100 | 0 | 1 | 0 |
| 9 | 68 | 90 | 10 | 5 | 85 | 5 | 5 | 10 |
| 10 | 32 | 100 | 0 | 1 | 90 | 5 | 5 | 3 |
| 11 | 13 | 80 | 20 | 1 | 99 | 0 | 0 | 9 |
| 12 | 8 | 90 | 10 | 0 | 95 | 0 | 0 | 5 |

*Key*
Others = Strangers, Other Family Members
1/y = Half Year

## Table 9
### Reason for Parental (Guardian)
### School Visitation (Actual Number) y

| Grade | Number of Students | Sports | Grades Unscheduled Conference | Fights with Students | Fights with Teachers | Transfer Student | Educational Matters |
|---|---|---|---|---|---|---|---|
| 7 | 36 | 0 | 0 | 7 | 3 | 36 | 0 |
| 8 | 45 | 0 | 0 | 3 | 3 | 45 | 0 |
| 9 | 68 | 0 | 2 | 16 | 6 | 68 | 0 |
| 10 | 32 | 0 | 1 | 0 | 7 | 32 | 0 |
| 11 | 13 | 2 | 1 | 0 | 2 | 13 | 0 |
| 12 | 8 | 0 | 1 | 0 | 2 | 8 | 0 |

*Key*
y = One School Year

## Schematic Analysis of the Problem

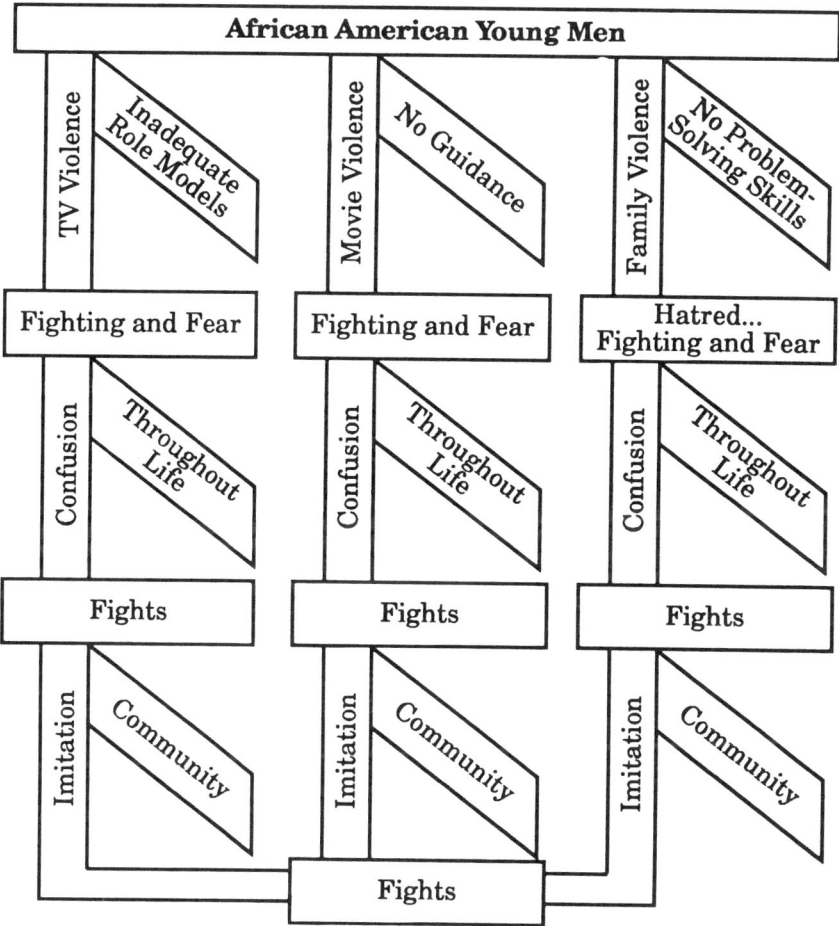

## African American Students
## Comments concerning fighting

1. "My mom says, 'Don't fight, shoot'"...S.J....9th grade.

2. "If someone hits me, I'm going to hit back"...S.B....9th grade.

3. "My mom says, If they look like they are going to hit me, hit first"...W.T....8th grade.

4. "My mom says if they hit you, come home and tell the family and they will go back and fix it"...H.Y....8th grade.

5. "I fight when people start with me"...A.B....7th grade.

6. "That is what I'm supposed to do"...H.D.G....11th grade.

7. "I only fight when they start with me"...E.M....7th grade.

8. "I just love to fight"...F.B....6th grade.

9. "My brother said that if I don't fight, he was going to beat me up"...J.B....10th grade.

10. "I will only fight when someone punch me first"...C.L.R....7th grade.

11. "My father said I better not come home after I lose a fight"...B.B....9th grade.

12. "My mother said that if I come home with my face all beat up, the other guy's face better be twice as bad"...R.W....10th grade.

13. "A boy who can't fight is less than a man"...N.L....12th grade.

During my studies some African American young men contributed this list of reasons for fighting:

1. To impress their friends.
2. To maintain a reputation.
3. To look important.
4. To impress their peers.
5. Because (as a statement).
6. To protect themselves.
7. To protect their friends.
8. To show heart (bravery).
9. They were called names.
10. To protect parents and relatives.
11. A gambling debt.
12. An attempt at extortion.
13. Being extorted.
14. Someone did not respect him.
15. Because he thought he could win.
16. The opponent was a punk.

## Expectations:

1. To educate people to understand the severity of the problem.

2. To reveal the negative influences fighting has on the educational process.

3. To allocate parental responsibility.

4. To allocate the perpetrator's responsibility.

5. To allocate schools' responsibilities.

6. To allocate community and governmental responsibilities.

7. To alleviate a problem that has decimated the African American culture.

8. To create a pleasant and safe home environment.

9. To create a pleasant and safe educational atmosphere for both students and teachers.

10. To foster African American male happiness and not despair.

## Recommendations

According to the information gathered by this investigator, there are numerous reasons for the fighting attitudes of the African American male. Listed below are some recommendations that will hopefully alleviate the reasons for these attitudes.

1. Parents should allow their children to express themselves. They should allow them to express themselves without interruptions. After they have finished expressing themselves, the parents may then challenge them, ask questions of them, agree with them, or correct them. It is the belief of this investigator, that if parents listen without interfering with the youngster, he will talk so frequently that he will answer impending questions before they are asked.
2. Parents should stop telling their children to fight back. They should realize that fighting back may sometimes cause more problems than the original situation called for. Oftentimes it may cause the death, injury, or incarceration of the persons originally involved in

the fight and also others, including family members. Perhaps turning the other cheek may not be such a bad idea (Shore, 1990).

3. Some African American young men believe that if they do not fight they are "punks." Parents should express their love to their sons and let them know that they would much rather have a live "punk" than a dead or severely beaten "brave son."

4. I recommend that African American parents nurture their sons throughout life (age 0-infinity). Some parents hug, kiss, and love their sons at a very early age. But oftentimes, for some unknown reason, as the sons grow older and larger the hugs and kisses are eliminated. This is a terrible mistake. Oftentimes these young men think they are being loved. But the hugs, kisses, and attention will reassure them. This show of affection should endure for a lifetime. Without it hostilities may begin to grow inside him and lashing out may become a part of his personality (Mcgraw, 1987).

5. All types of fighting and aggressive hostilities should be eliminated from the environment:
   (a) fight posturing;
   (b) television violence;
   (c) movie violence;
   (d) family fights.

6. I recommend that African American young men are taught phonics instead of fisticuffs.

7. I recommend that African American young men are taught that losing a fight or not fighting is not the end of the world.

8. African American young men should be taught at the ironic age not to be sensitive or easily embarrassed by insignificant things (Mcgraw, 1987).

9. I recommend that parents ostracize themselves and their children from anyone who sanctions fighting as an alternative to solving problems by peaceful means.

10. I recommend more extensive research in this area.

11. I recommend that domestic violence should cease at all costs.

12. I recommend the elimination of fighting from all schools. Horseplay and play fighting should also be eliminated.

## Comments from educators

The aggressive attitude that comes from students is not limited to African American males, but seems to cross all cultures and races. Because there are more African American men in specific locations, false generalizations may occur. The basis of the aggression shown in some African American males seems to stem from less self-esteem and manifests itself through negative behaviors: hostility, anger, impulsivity, and an indifference to learning. The aggressive behavior seems to stem from the frustration of not being able to learn the level of work, the presence of others who pick on the students, and stress brought from the home environment which many students carry like excessive baggage (P. Bell, 1992).

Boys tend to be more naturally aggressive in our culture. This, from my perspective, crosses all ethnic and social boundaries. If we are to use stereotypical assumptions in defining the aggressive tendencies of African American males, it becomes a self-fulfilling prophecy. If we expect these young males to be inherently aggressive, we treat them in that manner and expect them to fight. If we expect them to perform well in class and translate these positive expectations to them, they will. The unifying concept of all levels is high expectations. Translate that to the students and the fighting attitude of African American males will decrease (B. Uditsky, 1993).

# Section 8
## *African American Male Sexuality*

Most of my studies of sexuality have been about African American males. That is why this section will only concern the males. I will not discuss the females in detail because I am not yet comfortable with my knowledge of the subject. However some of this information may be helpful to the African American female.

Why this section? Why encourage parents to discuss African American male sexuality with their children? This author believes that a man who is sexually satisfied (which oftentimes can be accomplished in a second), and his mate who is sexually satisfied (which takes patience), will have tranquil lives. However if there is a relationship in which the female is not satisfied sexually and the male knows it, he is going to be one angry man. This is especially true if the male knows that his lack of knowledge and skill is the reason she is not satisfied. He will become jealous, extremely jealous, and if his problem is not corrected, he will in most cases become violent.

There are reasons that the African American male is inept in certain aspects of sexuality. There are reasons that he cannot sustain his ejaculation to at least give his female partner a chance at an orgasm through intercourse.

In his early sex life, his stolen sex was usually a quickie (fast). The speed was for fear of being caught. Watching animals and mimicking them was like going through a speed trap (except for the turtles). Everything was speed, speed, and hurry, hurry. Thus he had no time to make love. All he could do was ejaculate. What a terrible beginning.

James Whitley, 1975, compiled research on African American males who were incarcerated. His research showed that the inmates knew very little about their physical capabilities sexually and knew less of what it took to create an orgasm in a female. They all confessed that they had many female companions, and they all admitted that more times than not their intercourse sessions lasted three minutes or less. The history of African

American men on death row was sexually pathetic. They confessed that their intercourse sessions ranged from ejaculation almost before entrance, immediately upon entrance, and seconds after entrance.

William Brown, in 1977, studied the sensuous parts of the body that men explore. He found that when African American men discover a sensitively pleasing spot on the female (breast, clitoris, toes, navel, etc.) they overwork it, even to the point of boredom.

Research can be concluded in many directions. As far as I am concerned, this research supports my contention that sex plays a major part in the temperament, attitude, and behavior of an individual.

PARENTS, START TEACHING YOUR CHILDREN ABOUT SEX AT AN EARLY AGE.

Throughout the African American male's life he has had to accept the dubious reputation of being a Don Juan. He presumably had to play the role of a super-sexual expert who never failed to please a female sexually. He was coined as the stud who could persuade any woman to come to bed. Supposedly he had more sexual powers than all of the Greek Gods combined. And of course, he was the man with the grand genitals. The genitals that would make any man bow his head in shame when he looks at his own.

Most men of all races accept this myth about African American men. Most African American men accept this myth about themselves. They consider it their duty to pursue every woman available. Developing a lasting relationship that is meaningful is no consideration to most. They often, for shame, chase women like a male dog would chase a female dog in heat. It is oftentimes molded into their minds and hearts to assume this posture. They observe this type of behavior in their total environment—school, church, home, and places in which they socialize—and they follow suit. It is truly a way of life for some.

Men of different races oftentimes attempt to segregate their women from African American males because they think they have this sexual power of persuasion. Some think that the only reason they want to be around them is to have access to their women. This is evident in their attempt to segregate schools, social functions, and places of worship. Usually when an African American moves into a community that is not frequented by African Americans, members of the opposite race move out. It is not for fear of the man taking all of the jobs or job promotions. It is not the fear of him attaining better-looking homes. It is not the fear of him having an all-around better life style. In most cases, it is the fear of him using his superior sexual powers to seduce their women. Recurrently the attempt is made.

Who is at fault for this African American male attitude? This author believes that it is directed towards the most immediate environment, and the most immediate environment is controlled by the parents.

Most African American parents care little about the sexual knowledge of their sons. Their sex education at home is oftentimes limited to statements such as, "Boy, when you go out there you'd better put that thing on." They may make a statement such as, "If you go out there and get something, you are going to take care of it." Oftentimes when young boys have girlfriends who become pregnant, it's not really theirs, they just get the blame.

This is usually the limit of the African American male's sexual learning as a youngster at home. The remainder of his learning is from trial and error (it takes thirty years to learn using that method), porno books, and magazines. Television and movies provide some sex education, but most of it is bland. He also learns from the basic outlines that are offered in schools. Perhaps his first true lesson on sex was from watching animals. His friends usually offer some advice and education but his friends' knowledge is as limited as his.

There are basic foundations that should be built before the sexual encounter takes place, and these foundations are not taught by the mediums mentioned above. Teachers, clergy, professionals, sex therapists, and others can teach these foundations. But the parents have to be in the forefront, especially with the development of feelings.

First, he has to be taught to develop a personal and true relationship (home example). Second, he should be taught the value of honesty in a relationship (home). Third, he should be taught the value of caring for a single partner (home). Fourth, he should be taught the value of closeness (home). Fifth, he should be taught the value of sharing totally (home). And sixth, he should be taught to take a chance with one partner (home).

Usually the African American male will follow what he sees in his environment, if he observes the male figures in his life constantly pursuing women, he will probably mimic them. If he witnesses his mother being unfaithful to his father, given the chance he will probably be unfaithful to his mate. If his close friends are promiscuous, it is likely that he will be promiscuous.

Some women are responsible for some of the sexual shortcomings of the African American man. One example of this is the lies that they tell him about how good he is sexually. This sometimes happens immediately after intercourse, and sometimes during intercourse. Oftentimes the sexual sounds that a woman utters during the sex act encourages him to think that he is really doing what turns her on, when in fact he is not performing well at all. Women are oftentimes programmed to pretend that the man is performing correctly. But oftentimes this can turn on them later in the relationship. If she fakes pleasure, the man thinks he is doing everything correctly. He does not have anything to cultivate. He is doing it right.

It is sad to say that quite a few African American males have given up athletic opportunities because of what they have not been taught about human sexuality. They are afraid to change clothes or take a shower with other males on a particular team because they might have a small penis, small testicles, or few pubic hairs. They feel that if they cannot unfold big genitals in the locker room, it is embarrassing, so they will not participate. The same scenario goes for the young man in the high school gym locker room. Oftentimes they will not take gym and use other excuses. They will not become swimmers or gymnasts because the bulge in their pants won't be sufficient enough to impress the onlookers. Absurd!

This myth of super genitals and super-sexual powers must be stopped in its tracks. This idea of women-chasing and moving from family to family also must stop. African American males do not have the obligation to sexually please everyone approachable. And they should stop staring, whistling, and approaching every woman that comes by. Oftentimes they are trying to impress others. I often believe that if an African American man was standing on the street taunting a lady sexually, and she turned around and walked up to him with her dress up and invite him to take his penis out and penetrate her right there on the spot, first he would not take it out, and second, he would run.

Realistically the African American male's obligation lies with one female and himself. He should take the initiative to learn how to sexually please himself and his one female partner.

The burden is on the male to create wholesome attitudes about human sexuality and pass these positive attitudes on to his children. Hopefully they will continue the trend and pass them on to subsequent generations.

African American male, know thy self. Parents, help them to know themselves as sexual beings.

Some of the techniques that may increase the sexual arousal in the African American male may involve homosexuality, masturbation, oral sex, or on occasions all of the above. Each individual is unique and there is no one way to stimulate him or for him to respond to a stimulus. Because he responds on occasion in a certain way does not mean that the next time he will respond in the very same manner. Some women are so self-centered and not intent on how well they are stimulating the man, they are not really making love to him. They are holding a mirror to themselves and giving themselves a grade. They cannot forget themselves long enough to ensure male sexual arousal.

Just because the penis is erect does not mean that the man is ready to penetrate the vagina. Frequently women complain about their need for a slow hand, caresses, closeness, and attention. The African American male is no different. He needs all of the above and more.

The male nipple can become erect. This can be an important area of sexual stimulation for him. Although they are not as sensitive as the female's nipple, they are responsive and African American males want them kissed. The men should not hesitate to convey their sexual needs and desires to their sexual partner.

All of the skin of the male's body is sensitive and can be erogenous. He must communicate to his partner what feels good, how it feels good, how to touch him, and when to stop. Over-attention can become annoying.

Many women expect the man to be the great lover and to do all the preliminary caressing. It is most important to inform her that she would make love to him just as she would have him caress her.

Most African Americans love to have anilingus performed on them. They gain maximum pleasure from fellatio. Their problem is that they are oftentimes afraid to convey this to their sexual partner. The failure of the male to communicate his desires to his partner hampers both their sexual pleasure. To be a coward about this important part of his life is really to sexually enslave himself.

Remember, women are not mind readers, and most of them are self-centered after the sex act begins, and they don't consider the man, unless it is to complain about what they didn't obtain from the sex act.

Can you (male) remember being in a relationship and there were no complaints about the sexual aspect? And then all of a sudden you cannot do it right. All of a sudden there is a complaint about the duration of the act itself. Did you ever wonder why this was not brought up during the early experiences? One analogy is the one about making money. The more you make, the more you want. I think the same is true about females and lovemaking. The more you love them, the more they demand. Do not let their greed be a put-down to you.

If the African American male cannot create an orgasm in his mate, someone else will. It is very important that he understand the orgasm and the methods by which it is accomplished.

When engaged in a sexual encounter, the burden of female fulfillment is not entirely dependent on the male. It is on both partners. Some men and some women, as far as it is concerned, do not understand the orgasm. Some women have had as many as four children and never have experienced an orgasm. To add to the affliction, some women think they can ejaculate (come). Looking for misrepresentations in the male's presence during the sex act can adversely affect his libido. Men are more fortunate than women in climaxing, because men can have both orgasms and ejaculate. Women can have only orgasms. But the men should not boast about pleasure superiority because when women have an orgasm, it is greatly diffused.

Clitoral stimulation by penile thrusting, by oral or manual manipulation, evokes female orgasm which takes place deeper in the body around the vagina and other structures. When a female has an orgasm, it can come only through the clitoris. Where it ends no one knows, and it is so pleasurable to the female, she doesn't care. If the male is about to ejaculate (come) during penile thrusting and his female partner is not close to orgasm, she should be encouraged to masturbate. The male partner should watch closely, as to ascertain exactly where she likes to be touched—for future reference.

Frequently, and very early in life, the African American male is led to believe that if he does not have a big penis something is physically wrong with him. That is a fable that should be rapidly diminishing. The penis ranges from size small (a very small minority of men), medium (most men), large (some men), very large (a very small minority of men). There is an African American male that corresponds to all of these categories just as most other men do.

Masters and Johnson measured the penises of eighty men. The first group averaged 8 centimeters when flaccid and 16 centimeters when erect. The second group averaged 11 centimeters flaccid and 18 centimeters erect. The smaller flaccid penises tend to double in length with erection, while the longer flaccid group tend to lengthen about 80%. The African American male tends to appear in the group with the longer flaccid penis.

Parents, inform them that they are what they are and that they might as well get accustomed to it because what they have (genitals) at maturation (15-19) is what they will die with.

## Questions

Below is a list of questions that men from the ages of nine to twenty-two asked me about sexuality. These are not the exact words that they used but the essence of the questions did not change. I answered these questions as plainly as I could without crossing personal and/or religious barriers. PARENTS, these are some of the things your children wanted to know.

1. QUESTION. Why do some African American men like to have oral sex performed on them, but at the same time they don't want to perform oral sex on their partner?

    ANSWER. This is a classic example of selfishness and non-caring. However if this type of situation is explained to the female partner before the oral sex is performed on the male partner, it is perfectly fine.

2. QUESTION. What can you do when you know that you are not satisfying your partner sexually?

ANSWER. At times there is nothing you can do. But in most cases there is something that can be done. One thing you can do is to endeavor to develop a complete relationship with your partner and have sex as only a part of the total relationship. You should also learn about sexuality from experts in the field, and there are quite a few of them. Communication is of the utmost importance. Find out exactly what she likes sexually and find out where she likes to be touched. Discover whether or not she is orgasmic. Find out what she wants and deliver.

3. QUESTION. Are vibrators good to use on your female partner?

ANSWER. Vibrators are good to use sometimes in certain instances. Overuse can sometimes be very bad. Some females require more sustained clitoral stimulation before orgasm. This is a great help to some men because vibrators do not become fatigued.

4. QUESTION. Do women require the large penis?

ANSWER. Usually women who are orgasmic do not care what size the penis is, because a great majority of these women who are orgasmic prefer direct stimulation of the clitoris, either orally or manually. Nevertheless there are some women who do prefer the larger penis, but this is not to say that the larger penis is more orgasmically potent than a medium or small penis.

5. QUESTION. Do some women use anal intercourse as a surrogate form of coitus?

ANSWER. Some women enjoy having anal intercourse. Also some women have anal intercourse because their male partner enjoys it. Occasionally females enjoy it for its masochistic value. Quite a few engage in it because their monthly period is on or maybe there is some pain and/or trauma in the vagina.

6. QUESTION. Is it possible for a man to have intercourse with a woman who has a venereal disease and not catch the disease?

ANSWER. Only if the man is religiously lucky. The chances are a billion to one that he will catch it. The exception is granuloma inguinal.

7. QUESTION. Are handsome men more sensuous than less attractive men?

ANSWER. No man is more sensuous than another man merely based on how handsome he is. However the answer could be based on female preference.

8. QUESTION. Can any African American man be persuaded to go to bed with any good-looking woman?

ANSWER. Some African American men will go to bed with any good-looking woman. This is, among other reasons, because some of these men are constitutionally incapable of establishing a meaningful relationship with one woman. However some of them possess too much class to exhibit this type of behavior.

9. QUESTION. How would you solve the problem in which the female does not like having sex, but the male does, and they love each other?

ANSWER. You have one of three choices. You can attempt to change her attitude; you can become abstinent; or you can seek another female partner for your sexual gratification. Some females get paid for solving this type of problem. Oftentimes the female partner will have the strength to accept an arrangement that involves her mate having sexual relations with another woman. On the other hand some women will never accept it. This is the time to be honest with yourself and most of all it is the time to become realistic about your decision.

10. QUESTION. Do some women perform fellatio more freely than others?

ANSWER. Yes, most women know that African American males love fellatio (most all men actually), and it is oftentimes used to hold them. Some white women perform fellatio on African American men because they were taught that oral sex is not having sex per se. Some women readily use it to prevent pregnancy. And African American men have no complaints.

11. QUESTION. Can swallowing the ejaculate cause pregnancy in the female?

ANSWER. Positively no. The swallowed ejaculate goes inside the stomach, and the stomach is not the site of pregnancy.

12. QUESTION. Does male masturbation cause the penis to increase in size?

    ANSWER. No, the penis does not have the type of muscles in its shaft to cause it to enlarge from masturbation activity.

13. QUESTION. Does spitting in your urine following urination have anything to do with the ability to keep your female partner as long as you like?

    ANSWER. This is another in the long list of myths created in the African American community. The answer is absolutely no!

14. QUESTION. Do some African American males abnormally chase white females?

    ANSWER. Yes, for some unresolved reason, some men feel that white women have more to offer them than African American women. They oftentimes feel that they are more sophisticated than other women, another myth. It is also exciting to some because once they were the untouchables, but now they can have their fill. Some just want to experience the difference. All females are selected as to choice and outcomes vary with every race.

15. QUESTION. Is the size of the penis in the male analogous to the clitoris in the female?

    ANSWER. Yes, when the female become sexually excited the clitoris will become engorged with blood. When that happens it becomes thirty times its visible size.

16. QUESTION. Can a female ejaculate (come)?

    ANSWER. A female does not have the physical parts for ejaculation. However she does have orgasms. Oftentimes the fluids that you experience in and around her vagina are preliminary sexual fluids; accommodating fluids. These fluids allow easy and painless insertion of the penis.

17. QUESTION. Are all females orgasmic?

    ANSWER. No, but most females are, even some who don't think they are.

18. QUESTION. Are condoms used for the prevention of pregnancy or the prevention of venereal diseases?

    ANSWER. They are recommended for both, but they are better suited for the prevention of venereal disease because they sometimes break during penile thrusting. They sometimes develop small leaks. And they have been known to slip off.

19. QUESTION. Why do some African American men switch from female to female for their sexual gratification?

    ANSWER. Some African American males are not capable of engaging in a full and complete relationship with one woman. They are oftentimes afraid to take a chance on a relationship. Among some other things, they are afraid of their own sexual inabilities.

20. QUESTION. Do women have wet dreams?

    ANSWER. Women do not have wet dreams per se, however some women do have dreams that end in orgasm.

21. QUESTION. Does masturbation cause insanity, blindness, sterility, homosexuality, pimples, and does it demean your character?

    ANSWER. No, most people masturbate, even some married people masturbate. It is not abnormal, and it certainly will not cause any of the problems listed above. As a matter of fact most people, especially women, learn about their bodies through masturbation.

22. QUESTION. Why are some females excessively noisy during sexual intercourse, while others are calm and moderate?

    ANSWER. Some women fake sexual pleasure, and they do it with a lot of noise. They have that "You are hurting me syndrome." It is really a pathetic learned behavior. This behavior involves conveying to her sexual partner a sense of monumental sexual achievement. More often than not, she will be lying.

23. QUESTION. Who is responsible for teaching African American men about sexuality?

    ANSWER. Parents have the primary responsibility of teaching their children about sexuality, especially in their early years of development. But most parents either do not know about sexuality themselves or they are incapable of parting with this type of knowledge when it comes to their children. Schools, churches, libraries, older relatives (men and women), are very good sources of information. The reliable source other than experience is the trained sex therapist. The African American male should not think that this information will come to him. He should pursue the subject from all angles, but never take serious the information received from the boys on the corner.

24. QUESTION. Do African American males enjoy watching their lovers masturbate?

    ANSWER. Yes, very much so. When an African American male watches his partner masturbate, his own sensuousness is aroused many fold. Also by watching her, he will discover where and how she likes to be touched. The reverse situation is the same. When the female partner watches the male masturbate, especially when he nears ejaculation, she becomes highly excited. She wants to be the one to make him ejaculate.

25. QUESTION. Is there any food value in the male ejaculate?

    ANSWER. Doctors say that the male ejaculate contains protein, and protein is a quality food product.

26. QUESTION. Are women usually more capable and willing to develop and maintain a complete relationship with one person than men?

    ANSWER. Yes, women are more emotional than men, therefore they are more people-oriented. Men care more about situations while women care more about the feelings of situations.

27. QUESTION. Do women enjoy seeing men naked as much as men enjoy seeing women naked?

    ANSWER. Of course a woman enjoys seeing a man naked, especially during a sexual encounter, but under ordinary circumstances she can usually take it or leave it. Rather than seeing a man naked, a woman would rather have him say something nice to her. For example, "You look nice today. I love the smell of your perfume," or, "You are well dressed today."

28. QUESTION. Is there a relationship between masturbation and social level?

    ANSWER. Yes, masturbation is higher among higher socioeconomic groups. There are three major reasons. First, higher socioeconomic groups tend to have their first intercourse at a later age and therefore may practice masturbation longer. Second, masturbation requires imagination, and imagination is associated with educational status. Third, research suggests that sexual interest and activity levels are higher among higher socioeconomic groups with, therefore, a higher prevalence of all kinds of sexual behavior, including masturbation.

29. QUESTION. Why do some women continue to have unwanted pregnancies?

    ANSWER. Because of underlying unresolved conflicts which are being acted out with these pregnancies. Examples are substitutes for a missed parent or child, identification with her own parents or unborn child, and the male partner's strong desire to father a child. The less accepted view is the abject stupidity of the female.

30. QUESTION. What are some of the motives of African American men who rape women?

    ANSWER. Experts in the field say it is not a sexual crime. I tend to disagree. I am aware that other things such as masculinity doubts, psychological impairment, and the feeling of being in charge are important. But when a man sexually assaults a women, he is after sex.

31. QUESTION. Does Spanish fly work as an aphrodisiac?

    ANSWER. No! There are no real aphrodisiacs. They only exist in the minds of the people who want them to work.

32. QUESTION. Do more boys masturbate than girls?

    ANSWER. Yes, boys' sex organs are easily accessible and more visible than girls', and boys come into contact with their sex organs more often than girls.

33. QUESTION. Who do some female adolescents avoid using contraception?

    ANSWER. Adolescents are mostly cognitive and developmentally unready to make responsible use of the contraceptive.

34. QUESTION. Are there advantages of having sex with the lights on?

    ANSWER. Yes, the visual stimulus of looking at the genitals, the visual observation of the response to the stimuli, a greater opportunity for tactical foreplay, comfort and relaxation, and the acceptance of each partner's body are good advantages of having sexual relations with the lights on.

35. QUESTION. Why are some African American men offended when they are told "No" by a female?

    ANSWER. Because they consider the "No" a personal rejection of them, when in fact it is a simple refusal to engage in a sex act with them.

36. QUESTION. Is it possible to lose consciousness during sexual intercourse?

    ANSWER. Yes, heavy and deep breathing expels carbon dioxide from the lungs and decreases the amount of carbon dioxide in the blood. Blood vessels of the brain are dilated by carbon dioxide. If there is a deficiency of carbon dioxide in the blood, the blood vessels inside the brain will become constricted, thus creating a deficiency of blood flowing into the brain. This could cause unconsciousness.

37. QUESTION. Why do some African American men enjoy having sex with older women?

    ANSWER. There are many reasons for this behavior. One, she may be less demanding. Two, she may require less commitment. Three, she may be more knowledgeable about sex. Four, she may be less inhibited. And five, she may be more direct in expressing her own needs.

# Glossary

Below is a glossary of terms that may be helpful in your quest to teach your child about sex:

**ABORTION.** Applied more to intentional but also unintentional (more usually called miscarriage) premature ending of a pregnancy.

**ABSTINENCE.** To refrain from having sexual intercourse.

**AIDS.** (Acquired Immune Deficiency Syndrome), fatal disease caused by a virus known as HIV (human immunodeficiency virus). AIDS is primarily transmitted through sexual intercourse, but it can also be transmitted when contaminated blood comes in contact with a cut or break in the skin. The virus attacks certain types of white blood cells, leaving the body vulnerable to some kinds of infections and to cancers such as Kaposi's sarcoma. Symptoms include fever, drowsiness, skin infections, weight loss, swollen glands, weakness, headaches, and brown or purple nodules on the lower parts of the legs.

**AMBIVALENT.** The dual quality of conflicting mental and moral forces.

**ANAPHRODESIAC.** An agent that repels the stimulation of sexual passion.

**ANDROGEN.** A hormone that promotes the development and maintenance of the male secondary sex characteristics and structure.

**ANILINGUS.** Oral stimulation of the anus.

**APHRODISIAC.** An agent that stimulates sexual passion.

**ARTIFICIAL INSEMINATION.** A procedure in which a doctor inserts male semen into a woman's uterus to cause pregnancy when the women fails to conceive normally.

**ASEXUAL.** Having no sex.

**BISEXUAL.** A person who directs his or her sex drive toward both men and women.

**CASTRATION.** The surgical removal of the testes.

**CASTRATION ANXIETY.** Fear of the penis being bitten off.

**CELIBACY.** Abstaining from sexual intercourse for personal or religious reasons.

**CERVIX.** The lower part of the uterus. It is conical in shape and protrudes into the vagina.

**CHLAMYDIA.** A sexually transmitted disease (STD) considered to be the most common STD in the United States today.

**CLITORIS.** A small, erectile structure at the front of the female's vagina. It contains sexually sensitive nerves and corresponds to the penis.

**COITUS.** The act of sexual union.

**CONCEPTION.** Fertilization of an ovum by a sperm forming a zygote or fertilized egg which develops into an embryo.

**CONDOM.** Rubber covering worn over the penis to prevent venereal disease or conception.

**COPULATION.** The act of sexual union.

**CORPORA CAVERNOSA.** The space inside the penis that fills with blood during sexual excitement.

**CORYNE BACTERIUM VAGINALE.** Bacteria that causes foul-smelling menstruation fluids.

**COWPER GLANDS.** Two small glands discharging fluids into the male urethra.

**CUNNILINGUS.** The sexual stimulation of the vagina by using oral contact.

**DIALATOR.** An instrument used to wide or sustain an opening.

**DIAPHRAGM.** A form of birth control consisting of a soft rubber cap that covers the cervix to prevent entry of sperm.

**DIFFUSED.** To spread out over a large area.

**DILDO.** An artificial penis.

**DOUCHING.** Rinsing of the vagina with a liquid. It may be harmful unless prescribed for medical reasons.

**DYSFUNCTION.** An abnormality or impairment of function.

**DYSMENORRHEA.** Painful menstruation.

**DYSPAREUNIA.** Painful intercourse.

**DYSPHORIA.** The state of feeling unwell or unhappy.

**EJACULATION (COME).** The ejection of the seminal fluid from the male urethra.

**EJACULATION.** Ejection of semen.

**ELECTRA.** The close relationship a father might have with his daughter that can, but not necessarily, lead to sex.

**EMULATION.** To strive by imitation to equal others in accomplishment or quality.

**ENGORGE.** Swollen, hard.

**ENNUI.** Weariness, dissatisfaction.

**EPIDIDYMIS.** The greatly coiled sperm duct.

**ERECTION.** The hardening and enlargement of the penis caused by blood rushing into the tissue, usually during sexual excitement.

**EROGENOUS ZONES.** Areas of the body which, when touched, cause an increase in sexual excitement, including the lips, neck, ears, thighs, breasts, as well as the genitals.

**FECUNDATION.** The act of impregnating, fertilizing.

**FELLATIO.** Sexual stimulation of the penis by oral contact.

**FETISHISM.** Nonsexual things and parts of the body that arouse erotic feelings.

**FOREPLAY.** A term used to describe the caressing arousal that may lead to sexual intercourse.

**FRUSTRATION.** Incomplete, unfinished.

**GENITAL HERPES.** A viral sexually transmitted disease causing painful blisters that can recur through life.

**GENITALS.** The external sex organs.

**GLANS.** The distal end of the penis or clitoris.

**GONORRHEA.** A common sexually transmitted disease causing pain on urination and a discharge, especially in men.

**HARBINGER.** An indication of things to come.

**HETEROSEXUAL.** Preferring the opposite sex.

**HOMOSEXUAL.** Preferring the same sex.

**IMPOTENT.** The inability to have sexual intercourse, often caused by psychological reasons and sometimes physical deficiencies.

**INGRATING.** Constant givers.

**INTERJECTIONAL INTERCOURSE (INTERCOURSE).** Coitus, mating copulation, the sex act; the physical joining of male and female bodies, during which the penis is placed inside the vagina.

**INTROITUS.** The entrance to the vagina.

**IRRUMATE.** To suckle.

**LABIA.** The lips of the vagina.

**LESBIAN.** A female homosexual.

**LIBIDO.** Sexual desire, lust.

**MASOCHISM.** A type of sexual perversion in which a person receives pleasure from being dominated.

**MASTURBATION.** The act of self-stimulating the genitals to obtain sexual satisfaction.

**MICTURITION.** Urinating during sexual intercourse.

**MISSIONARY POSITION.** A sexual position in which the man is on top.

**NARCISSISM.** Refers to self love.

**NERVI ERIGENTES.** Maintains sexual functioning.

**NIPPLE.** The protuberance of the male and female breasts.

**NOCTURNAL EMISSION.** (Wet dream) a normal ejaculation of semen occurring during sleep.

**NPT.** Nocturnal penile tumescence.

**OEDIPAL.** The close relationship that a mother might have with her son that may or may not lead to having sex.

**ORCHIECTOMY.** The surgical removal of the testes.

**ORGASM.** The climax of sexual intercourse or masturbation.

**PAP SMEAR.** A technique developed chiefly by Dr. George N. Papanicolaou (1883-1962) that involves the microscopic examination of cells collected from the vagina. The Pap smear is an excellent technique for the early detection of cancer of the uterine cervix, or neck, of the womb. The Pap smear is one of the major reasons for the decrease in deaths from cancer of the uterine cervix.

**PENIS.** The male organ of copulation and semen transportation.

**PERIANAL.** Around and near all of the areas of the anus.

**PERINEAL.** Between the genitals and the rectum.

**PERISCROTAL.** Around and near all the areas of the testes.

**PHALLUS.** The penis or some other analogous organ.

**PHIMOTIC.** The tightness of the foreskin so that it can be drawn back over the glans.

**POTENCY.** The power of the male to perform the sex act.

**PREMATURE EJACULATION.** A situation in which a man reaches orgasm and ejaculates sooner than he wishes.

**PREPUCE.** The loose skin at the end of the penis.

**PROCTITIS.** The inflammation of the anus or rectum.

**PROSTATE GLAND.** The sex gland that produces semen.

**PROSTITUTE.** A person who sells sex for profit.

**REFRACTORY.** The waiting period after ejaculation.

**RETROGRADE.** Something that gets worse.

**SADISM.** The practice of a person who gains pleasure from hurting someone else.

**SATIETY.** Satisfaction beyond desire.

**SATYRIASIS (DON JUANISM).** Abnormal sexual craving in the male.

**SCROTUM.** The skin pouch below the penis that contain the two testes.

**SEMEN.** The thick, colorless fluid that contains hundreds of millions of sperm cells and is discharged from the urethra of the male during sexual excitement.

**SEMINAL VESICLE.** One of the two sacs that temporarily store semen.

**SPERM.** The reproduction cells in males.

**STEROID.** A sex hormone.

**TESTES.** Two sex glands that manufacture and store sperm cells.

**TUMESCENCE.** Swelling part, getting hard.

**URETHRA.** In the male, the tube that carries semen containing sperm cells.

**URTICARIA.** Bumps on the vulva.

**VAGINISMUS.** A small vagina, possibly caused by muscle spasms.

**VAS DEFERENS.** A long, thin duct that carries male sex fluids.

**VOYEURISM.** Abnormal and excessive interest in viewing sexual objects or activities.

**VULVA.** The external genital organs in women.

# Male Reproductive System
## Side View

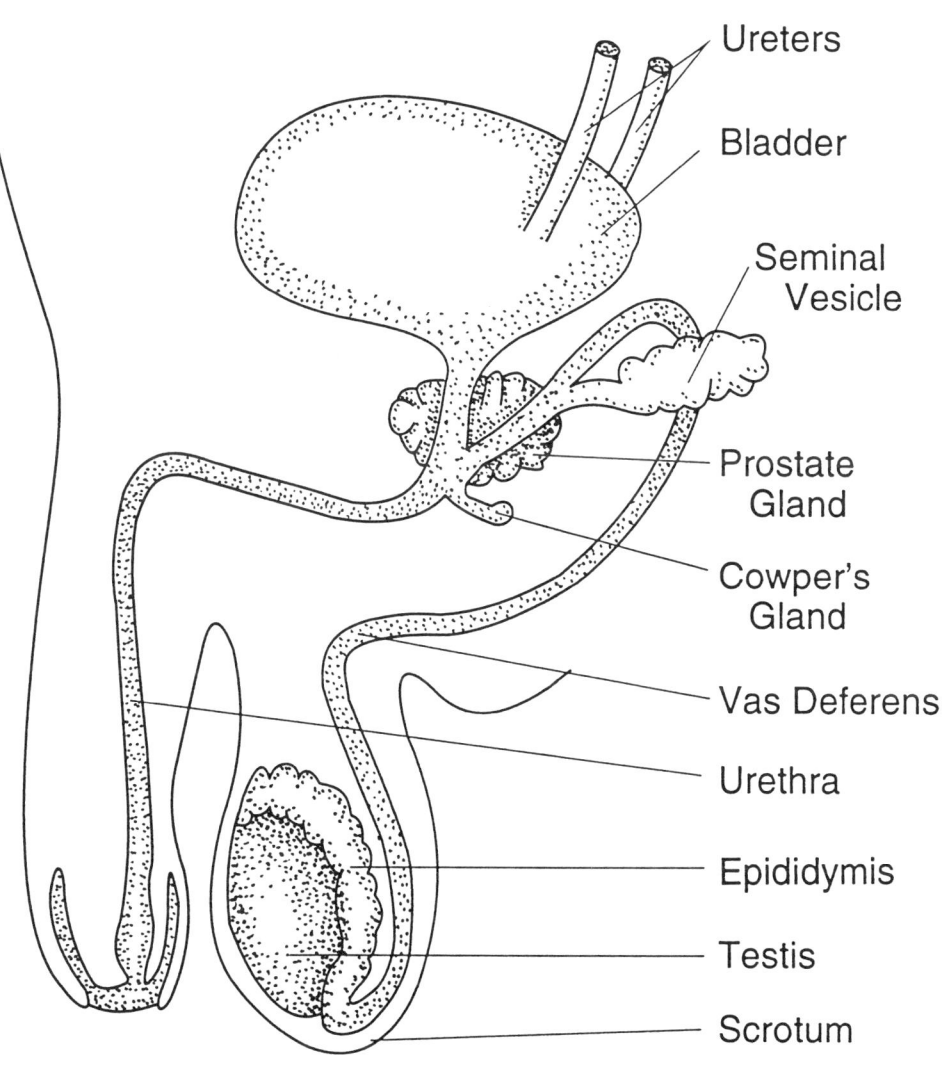

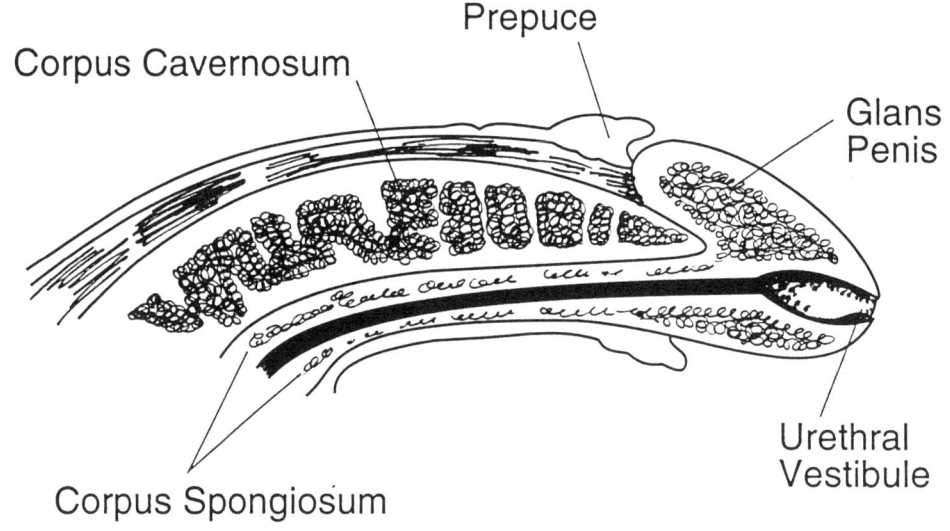

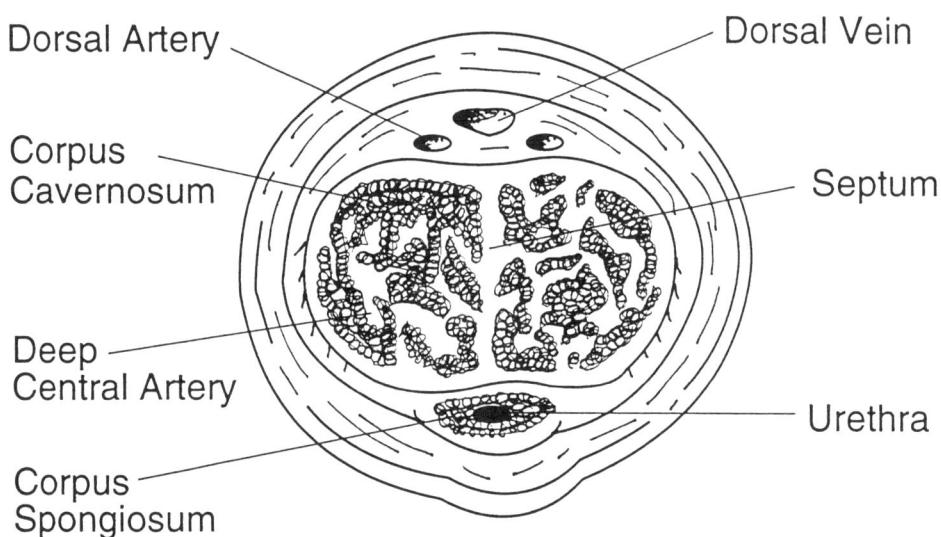

# External Female Organs

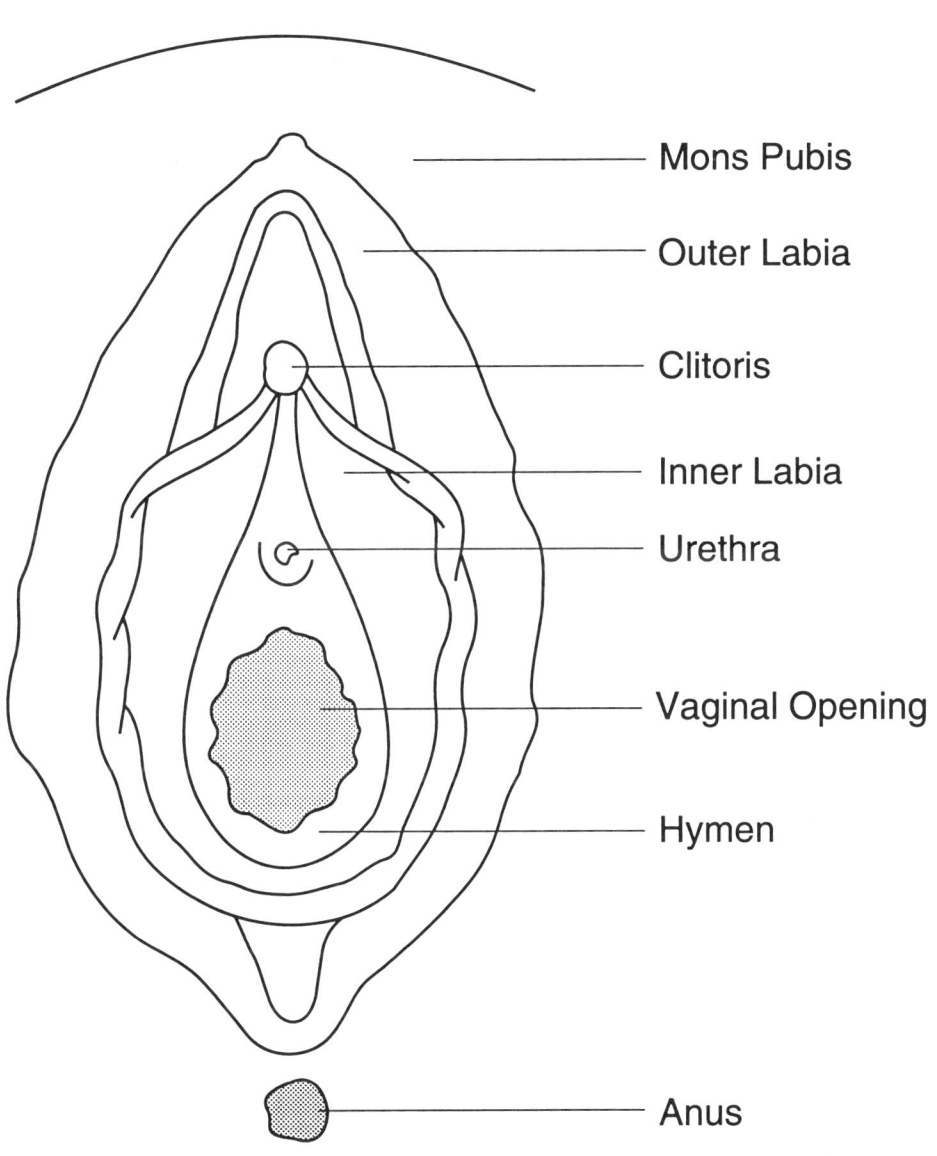

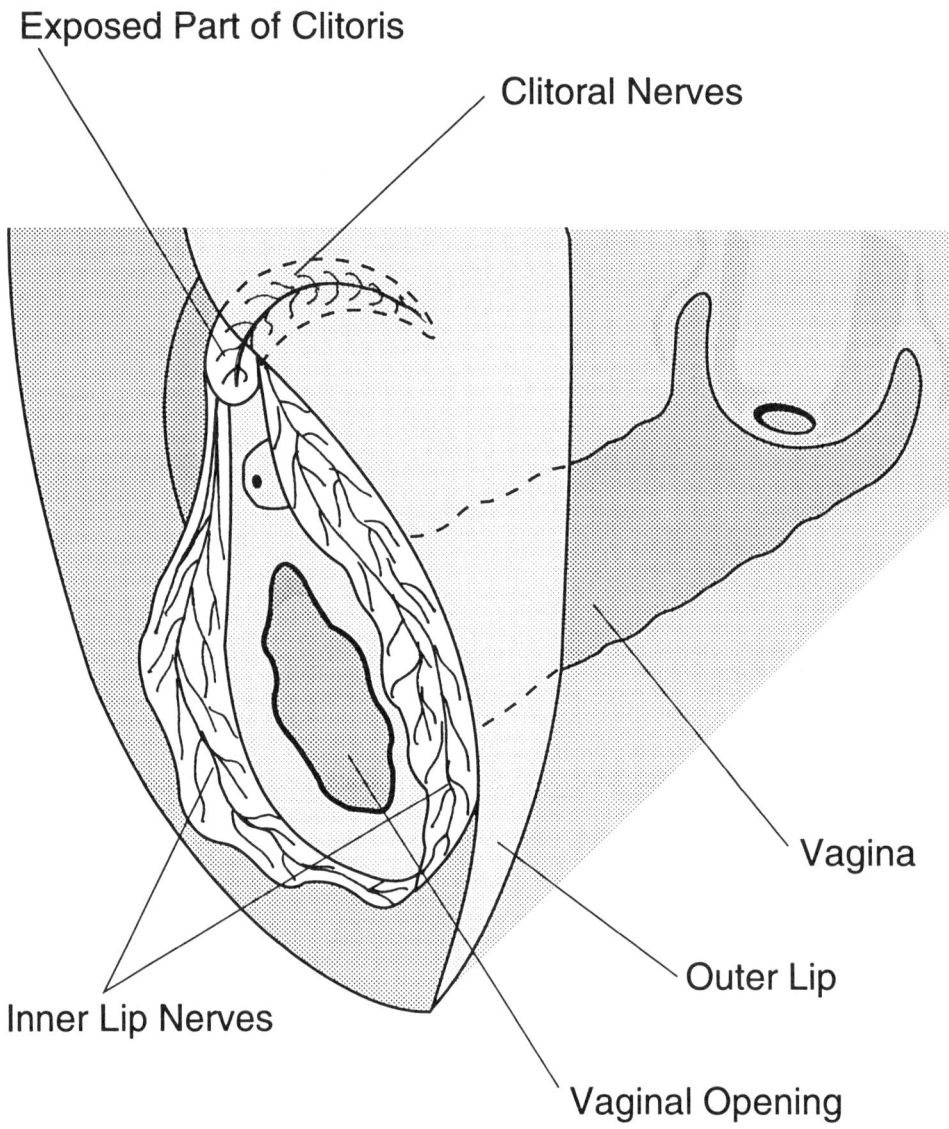

# Epilogue

In order to have a massive nationwide campaign for parenting (and I strongly recommend it), money is needed. And money is available if the people in power have the guts to use it and use it wisely. The federal government spends billions of dollars a year on such programs as "Get Set" and "Head Start." These programs are merely baby-sitting services. The federal government could use the same mechanisms and provide massive parenting classes throughout the nation. Parents will be paid to attend these classes. I also think the federal government is spending too much money on the AIDS epidemic. AIDS is something that can be prevented, and I don't think the federal government should empty its coffers for this program.

This author does not profess to have all of the answers necessary for successful child development. However it is my firm belief that some of the information within this book will be helpful if the parents, guardians, relative caregivers, or anyone entrusted with the responsibilities of raising children, would make an honest attempt to use it.

I am sure that many parental caregivers can personally identify with some of the parenting mistakes mentioned in this book. I only hope that they will not be deterred by that fact.